ServSafe Alcohol®

Fundamentals of Responsible Alcohol Service

National Restaurant Association
EDUCATIONAL FOUNDATION

DISCLAIMER

The information presented in this book has been compiled from sources and documents believed to be reliable and represents the best professional judgment of the National Restaurant Association Educational Foundation. The accuracy of the information presented, however, is not guaranteed, nor is any responsibility assumed or implied, by the National Restaurant Association Educational Foundation for any damage or loss resulting from inaccuracies or omissions.

Laws may vary greatly by city, county, or state. This book is not intended to provide legal advice or establish standards of reasonable behavior. Operators who develop beverage alcohol-related policies and procedures as part of their commitment to employee and customer safety are urged to use the advice and guidance of legal counsel.

Copyright Permissions
National Restaurant Association Educational Foundation
175 West Jackson Boulevard, Suite 1500
Chicago, IL 60604-2814
Email: permissions@nraef.org

Fundamentals with Exam Answer Sheet—FMX
ISBN 10: 1-58280-156-8
ISBN 13: 978-1-58280-156-8
Fundamentals without Exam Answer Sheet—FM
ISBN 10: 1-58280-161-4
ISBN 13: 978-1-58280-161-2
ISBN 978-0-471-71135-3 (Wiley Fundamentals with Exam Answer Sheet—FMX-W)
ISBN 978-0-471-71136-5 (Wiley Fundamentals without Exam Answer Sheet—FM-W)

Printed in the U.S.A.

10 9 8 7 6 5 4 3 2

Table of Contents

A MESSAGE FROM
The National Restaurant Association Educational Foundation

The National Restaurant Association Educational Foundation (NRAEF) is a not-for-profit organization dedicated to fulfilling the educational mission of the National Restaurant Association. Focusing on three key strategies of **risk management, recruitment,** and **retention,** the NRAEF is the restaurant and foodservice industry's premier provider of educational resources, materials, and programs. Proceeds from NRAEF products and services are invested directly back into the foundation in order to maintain and grow its world-class offerings, including ServSafe® food safety offerings and the ProStart® high school program.

Risk management is crucial to the success of every restaurant and foodservice operation. Serving alcohol responsibly is critical to preventing difficult circumstances in establishments, and ultimately, in the community. The NRAEF convened foodservice, regulatory, legal, academic, medical, and insurance experts to develop a new training program that focuses on what front-of-house employees need to know to serve alcohol responsibly.

By opening this book, you have made a significant commitment to responsible alcohol service. **ServSafe Alcohol®** is designed to train all members of an establishment including servers, hosts, valets, bouncers, coat checkers, etc. The program gives you information on understanding alcohol law and your responsibility, recognizing and preventing intoxication, checking identification, and handling difficult situations. You will also find places to record local laws and your company policies.

The NRAEF is dedicated to helping you serve alcohol responsibly. Additional materials to help you learn and retain responsible alcohol practices are:

- **Videos and DVDs.** Throughout the training course, videos/DVDs bring classroom material into real-world situations. Four of the videos/DVDs correspond to a respective chapter of the text. A fifth video/DVD will help you see challenging real-world scenarios involving guests who might be intoxicated, ID checking, and employees handling difficult situations.
- **Training throughout the organization.** Front-of-house training is vital to responsible alcohol service. The next step is responsible alcohol management. The NRAEF is currently creating training programs that reach all levels within an organization, which assist in creating consistent alcohol management objectives.

We applaud you for making the commitment to serving alcohol responsibly. Your training is a beneficial step toward making your operation and your community safe.

For more information on NRAEF and its programs, please visit **www.nraef.org.**

ACKNOWLEDGMENTS

The development of *Fundamentals of Responsible Alcohol Service* would not have been possible without the expertise of our many advisors, contributors, and manuscript reviewers. NRAEF is pleased to thank the following people for their time, effort, and dedication in creating the first edition of this book.

Adam Balick
Law firm of Balick & Balick

Jan Byrne
Alabama Alcoholic Beverage Control Board

Jack Carey
Aramark Corporation / Allstate Arena

Suzanne Carpenter
Carlson Restaurants Worldwide

Dimitrios Christopoulos
Law firm of Webster Wilcox Christopoulos, P.C.

Kat Cole
Hooters of America

Harry D'Ercole, Jr. and the staff of
Enrico's Italian Dining, Frankfort, IL

Pradeep Dudeja, Ph.D
University of Illinois at Chicago, Department of Physiology in Medicine

Mary Anne Ferrell
Darden Restaurants

Derek Fournier
Uno Restaurant Corp.

Nikki Fuchs
Buffalo Wild Wings

Steve Garrett
Garrett Photography

Scott Gellar Ph.D
Virginia Polytechnic University Center for Applied Behavior Systems

Tony Glavas and the staff of
The Courtyard Bistro, Frankfort, IL

Commander Tim Goergen
Bloomingdale, IL Police Department

Robert Gomez
Subterranean Nightclub

Ken Hirsch
CNA E&S Insurance

Vicki Houston
Damon's International

Roger Johnson
Wisconsin Department of Revenue, Alcohol & Tobacco Enforcement Division

Brian Kringen
Minnesota Department of Public Safety

Kenneth and Jillian Kukla and the staff of
Jackson's Bar & Grill, St. John, IN

Lydia R. Menzel, Ed.D
Performance Partnership, Inc.

Jennifer Michaud
CHAMPPS

William Miller, Ph.D
University of New Mexico, Department of Psychology

Ron Molk
Classic Images

Shalon Morris
Carlson Restaurants Worldwide / TGI Friday's

Lee Roupas
Illinois Liquor Control Commission

Kathy Rusnacko
Famous Dave's of America

Warren Sackler, CHA, FMP
Rochester Institute of Technology, Hospitality and Service Management Department

Chief Darrell Sanders, Ret.
Frankfort, IL Police Department

Christine San Juan
Bertucci's Corporation

Robert Schaefer
Bennigan's

Angie Simmons
CHAMPPS

Steve Skonecke and the staff of
Kansas Street Grill, Frankfort, IL

Michael Storm
Harrah's Casino, Joliet, IL

Traci Toomey, Ph.D
University of Minnesota, School of Public Health

Rich and Sara Tucker
Product Evaluations, Inc.

James Webster
Law firm of Webster Wilcox Christopoulos, P.C.

Viage ID reader courtesy of CardCom Technology

I.D. Checking Guide
courtesy of The Drivers License Company

HOW TO USE
Fundamentals of Responsible Alcohol Service

Suggested below is a plan for studying and retaining the responsible alcohol service knowledge in this textbook that is vital to protecting you, your guests, and your establishment.

Beginning Each Chapter

Prepare for the section by completing the following:

- **Review the Learning Objectives.** Located on the front page of each chapter, the learning objectives identify tasks you should be able to do after finishing the chapter. They are linked to the essential practices for serving alcohol responsibly.
- **Test Your Knowledge.** Before you begin reading, test your prior knowledge of some of the chapter's concepts by answering five True or False questions. If you want to explore the concepts behind the questions further, see the page references provided. Answers are located at the back of each chapter.

Throughout Each Section

Use these features to help you identify and reinforce the concepts in the chapter:

- **Concepts.** These topics are important for a thorough understanding of responsible alcohol service. They are identified before the introduction to each chapter.
- **Graphics.** Placed throughout each chapter to visually reinforce the key concepts in the text, they include charts, photographs, illustrations, and tables.
- **Something to Think About.** Based on real-world examples, these stories reveal the potential impact of careless alcohol service.
- **How This Relates to Me.** Throughout each chapter, there are opportunities for you to write in information specific to your location or operation, such as alcohol-related laws or company policies. If you are training in a group, your instructor may provide this information; if you are training with your manager or studying independently, you should research these topics to ensure you have the most appropriate information for your jurisdiction.
- **Activities.** Apply what you have learned by completing the various activities throughout each chapter. In Chapters 2, 3, and 4, you will have the opportunity to apply what you have learned by viewing and responding to scenes presented in a video corresponding to this text called *Evaluating Real-World Scenarios.* Completing the activities featured in this video/DVD is required for this course. Answers for activities are located at the back of each chapter.

At the End of Each Section

Once you have finished reading and completing the activities throughout each chapter, see how well you have learned.

- **Answer the Multiple-Choice Study Questions.** These questions are designed to test your knowledge of the concepts presented in the chapter. If you have difficulty answering them, you should review the content further. Answers are located at the back of each chapter.

ILLINOIS

1 Alcohol Law and Your Responsibility

After completing this chapter, you should be able to:

- Identify criminal liability as it relates to the sale and service of alcohol.
- Identify criminal violations related to the sale and service of alcohol and their consequences.
- Identify civil liability as it relates to the sale and service of alcohol.
- Define dram shop law.
- Recognize the impact of employee violations on the owner and the establishment and identify consequences.
- Identify the role of the liquor authority.
- Identify liquor authority violations and their consequences.
- Identify laws restricting alcohol service.

Note: The information provided is intended only to inform and assist the reader in understanding basic areas of alcohol law and the responsibilities involved therein. The information provided should not be considered legal advice, nor is it intended to address how particular laws may apply to a problem that might arise. The reader is encouraged to discuss any specific problem with appropriate counsel before making any decision with respect to the matters discussed or the information provided in this chapter.

TEST YOUR KNOWLEDGE

1. **True or False:** You may be charged with a crime simply for serving a guest who appears to be intoxicated. *(See page 1-4.)*
2. **True or False:** It is illegal to serve alcohol to a pregnant woman. *(See page 1-9.)*
3. **True or False:** Dram shop laws protect the server from being sued in the event that an intoxicated guest injures another individual. *(See page 1-5.)*
4. **True or False:** The state liquor authority can suspend an establishment's liquor license for allowing a minor to enter the establishment with a fake ID. *(See page 1-6.)*
5. **True or False:** All guests must be 21-years old to purchase alcohol. *(See page 1-8.)*

For answers, please turn to page 1-12.

CONCEPTS

- **Criminal liability:** Being held responsible for committing a crime. Servers can be held criminally liable for violating state, county, or municipal alcohol service laws, particularly for serving someone under 21 years of age or serving someone who is intoxicated.

- **Civil liability:** Being held responsible for payment of damages for injuring a person. Servers can be sued and forced to pay damages if their actions or lack of care while serving alcohol lead to an injury.
- **Dram shop laws:** Laws that allow an establishment and its owners and employees to be sued by someone injured by a patron who had been drinking alcohol at the establishment.
- **Liquor authority:** State or municipal agency that enforces alcohol regulations and licensing laws.

YOUR RESPONSIBILITY AS A SELLER OR SERVER OF ALCOHOL

As a member of the service staff, you must understand your liability regarding alcohol service. Being liable means you have legal responsibilities. If you do not act in accordance with the law, you could face consequences ranging from lawsuits to criminal charges—which could result in fines or even imprisonment. In addition, your establishment could lose its liquor license and be forced to close. You must always balance the desire to please your guests with your legal responsibilities regarding alcohol service. Sometimes the customer is not always right.

Cert

This chapter will give you a better understanding of general alcohol laws and how they directly impact you.

SOMETHING TO THINK ABOUT...

The following is based on a true story.

It was a busy Saturday evening at a club in a small Midwestern town. One of the establishment's regulars sat quietly at the bar. The bartender poured the man his favorite drink, and then moved along to fill the drink orders from the servers attending to the rest of the crowd. As the night progressed, the bartender kept an eye on the glass of his regular, ready for the man's signal to fill it again.

About two hours later, showing no signs of intoxication, the regular left. He got in his truck to drive the two miles from the club to his house. Five minutes after leaving the establishment, he crashed his truck into a car carrying two 20-year old college students. All three were killed. In the subsequent investigation, it was discovered that the man had consumed a fifth of liquor in the two hours he was at the club, or the equivalent of 17 drinks.

In a civil suit brought by the students' parents, the owners of the club were ordered to pay $500,000 to the families. The establishment also lost its liquor license and was forced to close. In addition, the bartender was tried and convicted of criminal recklessness, and given the maximum penalty. He was ordered to serve 180 days in jail, as well as pay a fine. He was also required to pay the court costs of the families. Lastly, as a condition of his sentence, the judge ordered the bartender to place a picture of the deceased students in his jail cell for the length of his term.

Criminal Liability

As a seller or server of alcohol, you may face criminal charges if you break state, county, or municipal alcohol laws.

Most states may hold you criminally liable for the following actions:

- Serving alcohol to a minor
- Serving a guest who is or appears to be intoxicated
- Possessing, selling, or allowing the sale of drugs on the premises

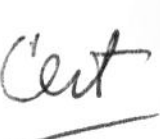

The consequences of these violations can be serious. Depending on the state in which you work, you could be placed on probation, fined, or even given jail time. In Illinois, for example, selling or serving alcohol to a minor is a Class A misdemeanor punishable by a fine of up to $2,500 and a jail sentence of up to one year.

SOMETHING TO THINK ABOUT...

A new law in New Mexico went into effect on July 1, 2004, making it a felony to purchase, give, or sell alcohol to anyone under the age of 21. Each violation could result in 18 months in jail and a $5,000 fine. This is the first law in the U.S. that imposes felony charges on those who provide alcohol to a minor.

Civil Liability

You have probably heard of establishments that have been sued by guests who were injured on the premises, but did you know that bartenders and servers have also been sued because they contributed to a guest's injury or did nothing to prevent it? Your civil liability as a seller or server of alcohol means you can be held responsible for payment of damages in addition to criminal charges.

Many states have passed dram shop laws, which create a special kind of civil liability for establishments with liquor licenses and for the people employed by them. These laws allow someone—who may not have been in the establishment—to sue the business, its owners, and its employees for injuries caused by a guest who was drinking there.

During any civil lawsuit, the court will look at the actions you took at the time of the incident in question. Did you check your guest's ID? Did you stop serving because the guest was becoming intoxicated? The "atmosphere" of the establishment will also be questioned. Do servers check IDs at all times? Are guests allowed or even encouraged to become intoxicated? Are policies in place to protect guests' overall safety? It is crucial for you to learn how to serve alcohol responsibly to your guests. It is even more important to be aware, be consistent, and apply your knowledge of responsible service on the job—for your protection and for the protection of your guests.

SOMETHING TO THINK ABOUT...

The following are based on true stories.

Driving home from a party at a friend's house, a couple on their motorcycle was struck by an oncoming car. The man on the motorcycle broke every bone in his left leg, from foot to hip. His wife, seated behind him, suffered a severe pelvic injury, rendering her unable to have children.

Upon investigation, it was revealed that the driver of the car had recently left a private party at a local, casual-dining establishment. In civil court, the couple sued the restaurant for serving a guest who was visibly intoxicated. During the trial, a subpoenaed server testified that she knew the driver of the car had been drunk, but had continued to serve him anyway. The jury found in favor of the couple, awarding them $39 million in damages.

In another case, a 25-year old woman drove her car into a utility pole soon after leaving a small pub. According to the coroner's report, her BAC was twice the legal limit. Based on that information, the woman's family named the bar's owners and the bartender in a civil lawsuit, seeking over $25,000 in damages. It was subsequently revealed that at no point did the bar stop service to the woman, despite knowing she was driving home.

THE ROLE OF THE LIQUOR AUTHORITY

Every state has its own liquor laws and oversees the sale and service of alcohol within its borders. Laws vary considerably from state to state. To complicate matters further, many counties and towns have their own, often stricter, liquor laws.

Each state and many municipalities have a liquor authority—often called the Alcoholic Beverage Control or Liquor Control Commission—that enforces alcohol laws along with the local police. In addition, these agencies are responsible for issuing and monitoring liquor licenses, issuing citations for violations, and holding hearings for violators of the liquor code.

HOW THIS RELATES TO ME...

In my state/municipality, my liquor authority is

PA LCB

Obtaining a liquor license is not a right, but a privilege granted to establishments meeting specific conditions. Citations can be issued to the owner and/or their employees if these conditions are violated.

The liquor authority can issue citations for the following violations:

- Selling liquor to a minor
- Failing to check identification of a guest who appears to be underage
- Allowing a minor to enter the establishment with a fake ID
- Serving a guest who is or appears to be intoxicated
- Discriminating against patrons due to race, gender, age, or sexual orientation

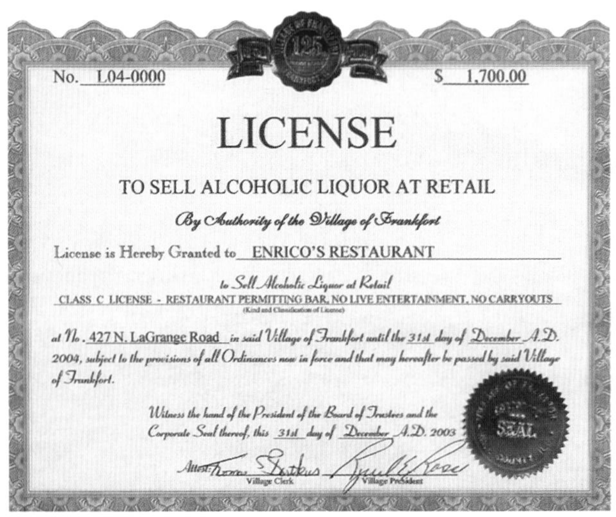

No. L04-0000 $ 1,700.00

LICENSE

TO SELL ALCOHOLIC LIQUOR AT RETAIL

By Authority of the Village of Frankfort

License is Hereby Granted to ENRICO'S RESTAURANT

to Sell Alcoholic Liquor at Retail

CLASS C LICENSE - RESTAURANT PERMITTING BAR, NO LIVE ENTERTAINMENT, NO CARRYOUTS

(Kind and Classification of License)

at No. 427 N. LaGrange Road in said Village of Frankfort until the 31st day of December A.D. 2004, subject to the provisions of all Ordinances now in force and that may hereafter be passed by said Village of Frankfort.

Witness the hand of the President of the Board of Trustees and the Corporate Seal thereof, this 31st day of December A.D. 2003

Attest: Village Clerk Village President

SEAL

A liquor authority violation can result in the suspension or revocation of the establishment's license.

- Selling or serving alcoholic beverages at those times or occasions when it is not permitted

Cooperate when law enforcement enters your establishment.

These violations can result in a fine for both the server and the owner, and suspension or revocation of the establishment's liquor license—putting the operation out of business. In states that license servers to serve alcohol, the state may also take away the server's license.

Liquor authorities can enter establishments at any time without notice. State liquor laws require you to cooperate when law enforcement agents or agents of the liquor authority visit your establishment. Be polite, and immediately notify your manager.

SOMETHING TO THINK ABOUT...

Compliance checks, or stings, are a common way for the liquor authority and local law enforcement to monitor the service of alcohol to underage drinkers. Working with undercover teenage volunteers, police monitor their attempts to buy alcohol with minor IDs, or sometimes with no identification at all. In one recent check in New York, the volunteers, ranging in age from 16 to 18, were able to buy a drink from one out of every three servers they approached. Over 40 servers were arrested and charged during the three-day operation, each facing $1,000 fines and up to a year in jail.

LAWS RESTRICTING ALCOHOL SERVICE

Since laws pertaining to the sale and service of alcohol vary widely, you must become familiar with those that apply to your establishment. These may include the following:

1. **Legal age to drink:** In all 50 states, an individual must be 21-years old to purchase alcohol. In some states, it is currently legal for a parent or legal guardian to purchase alcohol and serve it to a minor child.
2. **Legal age to serve:** In general, you must be 21-years old to serve alcohol. However, this law varies. For example, some states allow underage servers to bring alcohol to the table but not to pour it. Others allow underage servers to take the order and payment for the drink, but not to serve the order. Some states require the underage server to apply to the liquor authority for permission to serve alcoholic beverages.

HOW THIS RELATES TO ME...

In my state/municipality, you must be: __18__ years old to serve alcohol.

__18__ years old to pour alcohol.

__18__ years old to take a drink order.

3. **Legal age to enter the establishment:** In some areas, the law does not allow minors to enter a tavern or restaurant bar area. Some establishments may require guests to be older than the age allowed by law to enter the bar.

HOW THIS RELATES TO ME...

At my establishment, minors are (allowed/not allowed) __________ inside.

At my establishment, a guest must be __________ years old to enter.

At my establishment, minors are (allowed/not allowed) __________ in the bar area.

4. **Serving intoxicated guests:** It is illegal to serve a guest who is intoxicated or who shows signs of intoxication. (In Chapter 2, you will learn how to identify visible signs of intoxication.)

5. **Serving a pregnant guest:** It is illegal to deny alcohol service to a woman because she is pregnant. This would be considered gender discrimination. Many states, however, require establishments to post signs warning about the effects of alcohol on a fetus.

It is illegal to serve an intoxicated guest.

HOW THIS RELATES TO ME...

In my state/municipality, warning signs about the effects of alcohol on a fetus (are/are not) __________ required.

6. **Hours of service:** The legal hours for the sale and service of alcohol are listed in the establishment's liquor license and must be strictly followed.

HOW THIS RELATES TO ME...

I cannot sell or serve alcohol before __________ (a.m./p.m.) at my establishment.

I must stop selling or serving alcohol at __________ (a.m./p.m.) at my establishment.

7. **Happy hours and other drink promotions:** Some states, counties, and municipalities restrict or forbid "happy hours" and other drink promotions.

   These laws may prohibit serving a guest

   - two or more drinks at a time.
   - an unlimited number of drinks for a fixed price.
   - reduced-priced drinks for a specified period of time.
   - drinks containing additional alcohol without an increase in price.
   - drinks as a prize for a game or contest conducted at the establishment.

HOW THIS RELATES TO ME...

Restrictions on drink promotions in my jurisdiction include:

No 2 for 1 - price specials only

For information on your state's law concerning the sale and service of alcohol, visit the National Restaurant Association Educational Foundation's Web site at **www.nraef.org/reg_require.**

SUMMARY

It is important that all service staff understand their legal responsibilities, or liability, regarding alcohol service. As sellers or servers of alcohol, you should be concerned with two types of liability: criminal and civil.

You can face criminal charges if you break state, county, or municipal alcohol law, such as serving alcohol to a minor, serving a guest to the point of intoxication, or serving an already intoxicated guest. Depending on the state in which you work, you could be placed on probation, fined, or given jail time.

Your civil liability as a seller or server of alcohol means you can be held responsible for payment of damages in addition to criminal charges. Many states have passed dram shop laws, which create a special kind of civil liability for establishments with liquor licenses. These laws allow someone who may not have been on the premises to sue the establishment, its owners, and its employees for being injured by a guest who was drinking there.

Every state has its own liquor laws and oversees the sale and service of alcohol within its borders. Since these laws vary, you must become familiar with those that apply to your establishment.

Each state and many municipalities have a liquor authority that enforces alcohol laws. In addition, these agencies are responsible for issuing and monitoring liquor licenses, issuing citations for violations, and holding hearings for violators of the liquor code. Citations for violating liquor licensing laws can result in a fine for both the server and the owner and suspension or revocation of the establishment's license—putting the operation out of business. In states that license servers to serve alcohol, the state may take away the server's license.

MULTIPLE-CHOICE STUDY QUESTIONS

?

1. **State or municipal liquor authorities can issue citations for**
   A. drunk driving.
   B. serving a pregnant woman.
   C. serving alcohol to a minor.
   D. All of the above

2. **Dram shop laws**
   A. protect servers from lawsuits.
   B. protect establishments from lawsuits.
   C. release servers from criminal liability related to liquor code violations.
   D. allow a person to sue an establishment for being injured by an intoxicated guest.

3. **Which of the following is a criminal violation related to the sale and service of alcohol?**
   A. Serving alcohol to a minor
   B. Witnessing a drug transaction and failing to report it to law enforcement
   C. Serving a guest who appears to be intoxicated
   D. All of the above

4. **Luis serves Eddie five glasses of wine over the course of an hour at The Baldwin Grill. While driving home, Eddie hits an oncoming car, injuring the other driver. Under dram shop law, who other than Eddie can be held liable in a civil suit brought by the injured driver?**
   A. Luis
   B. The Baldwin Grill
   C. Marco and Theresa Baldwin, owners of the restaurant
   D. All of the above

5. **All of the following are possible consequences for violating the liquor code *except***
   A. fines.
   B. jail time.
   C. loss of building permit.
   D. suspension of the liquor license.

For answers, please turn to page 1-12.

ANSWERS

Page	Activity
1-2	Test Your Knowledge
	1. True
	2. False
	3. False
	4. True
	5. True
1-11	Multiple-Choice Study Questions
	1. C
	2. D
	3. D
	4. D
	5. C

NOTES

Recognizing and Preventing Intoxication

After completing this chapter, you should be able to:

- Identify alcohol's path through the body.
- Identify the liver's role in breaking down alcohol in the body.
- Identify factors that affect a guest's BAC.
- Identify drinks that contain the same amount of alcohol.
- Identify how to count drinks accurately.
- Identify the physical and behavioral signs of intoxication.
- Identify methods for preventing guests from becoming intoxicated.

TEST YOUR KNOWLEDGE

1. **True or False:** A lean guest will become intoxicated faster than a guest with a high percentage of body fat. *(See page 2-6.)*
2. **True or False:** A 12-ounce beer contains less alcohol than one-and-a-half ounces of 80-proof vodka. *(See page 2-12.)*
3. **True or False:** The liver can break down alcohol at the rate of two drinks per hour. *(See page 2-5.)*
4. **True or False:** Carbohydrates are the best type of food to serve with alcohol to help prevent intoxication. *(See page 2-25.)*
5. **True or False:** A guest who switches to larger or stronger drinks may be intoxicated. *(See page 2-19.)*

For answers, please turn to page 2-30.

CONCEPTS

- **Blood Alcohol Content (BAC):** Amount of alcohol that has been absorbed into the bloodstream, expressed as a percentage.
- **Small intestine:** Organ from which the majority of consumed alcohol is absorbed into the bloodstream.
- **Liver:** Organ responsible for breaking down alcohol in the body at a constant rate of one drink per hour.
- **Tolerance:** Drinker's ability to endure the effects of alcohol without exhibiting signs of intoxication.
- **Proof:** Measure of a liquor's strength. The percentage of alcohol in a liquor can be determined by dividing its proof in half.

ALCOHOL AND THE BODY

To protect your guests, you must understand how alcohol moves through the body, how it is eliminated, and the factors that affect its concentration in the bloodstream. This information will make it easier to understand what you can do to prevent intoxication.

Alcohol's Path through the Body

Alcohol moves through a person's body in much the same way as food. Unlike food, however, it does not need to be digested in order to reach the bloodstream. How does alcohol reach the bloodstream? To find out, let's take a closer look at what happens when a person drinks alcohol.

1. Mouth
A small amount is immediately absorbed into the bloodstream through the mouth.

2. Stomach
From the mouth, the alcohol moves into the stomach where some is absorbed into the bloodstream through the stomach wall.

3. Small intestine
From the stomach, the alcohol moves to the small intestine, where most of it is absorbed into the bloodstream.

4. Throughout the body
Once in the bloodstream, alcohol travels quickly throughout the body, reaching organs—including the brain—in minutes.

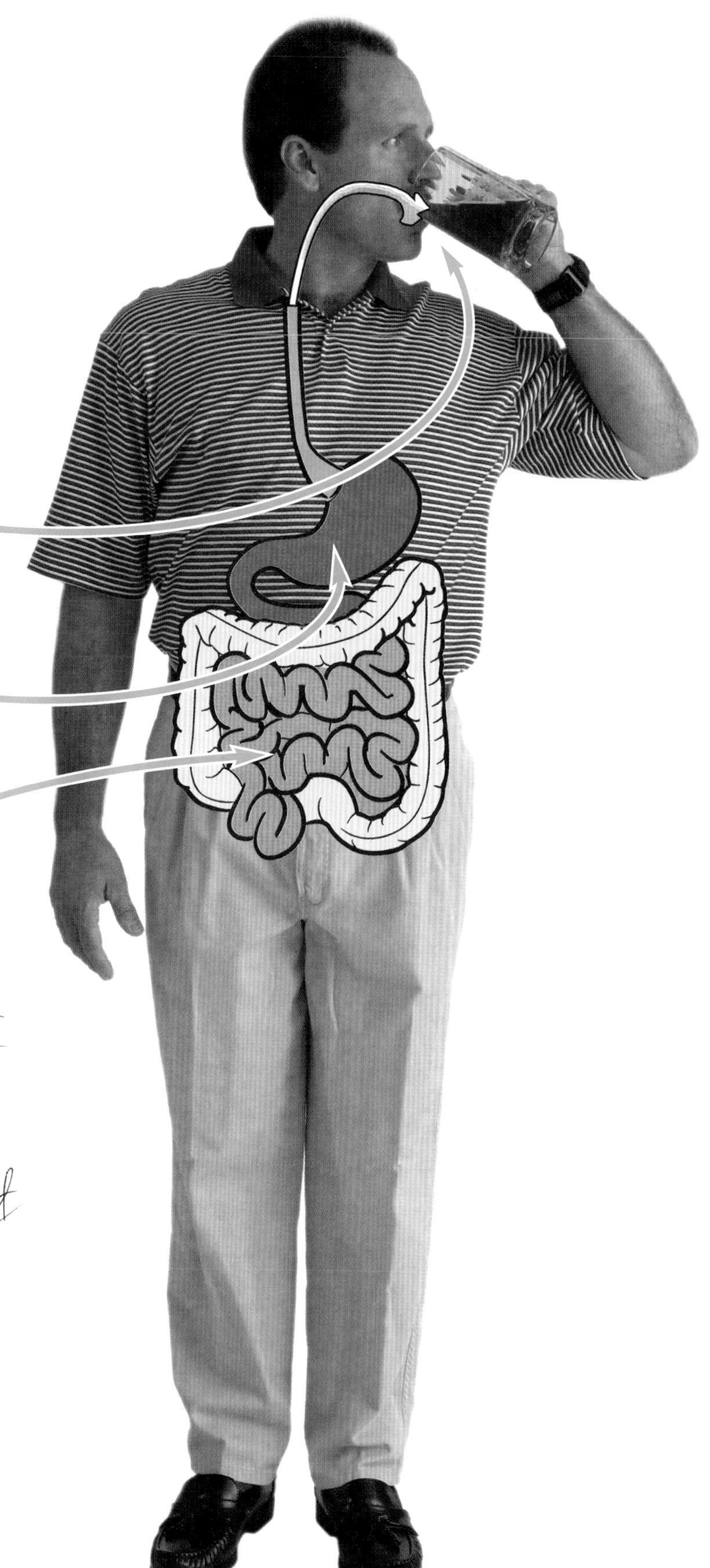

The amount of alcohol that has been absorbed into a person's bloodstream is called Blood Alcohol Content (BAC). A BAC of .10 means there is about one drop of alcohol present for every 1000 drops of blood. In all 50 states, it is against the law to drive with a BAC of .08 or higher. A BAC of .30 or higher can lead to coma or death.

SOMETHING TO THINK ABOUT...

Recently, a 19-year old college sophomore died after consuming the equivalent of 40 beers in an 11-hour period. Her BAC was .43—more than five times the legal limit for driving.

APPLY YOUR KNOWLEDGE: *Believe It or Not?*

Place an X next to each activity that removes a large amount of alcohol from the body.

1.____ Breathing

2.____ Drinking coffee

3.____Taking a cold shower

4.____ Exercising

5.____ Urinating

For answers, please turn to page 2-30.

The Liver's Role in Removing Alcohol from the Body

Actually, none of the activities in the *Believe It or Not?* exercise will eliminate a significant amount of alcohol from the body. Only the liver can break down alcohol. It does this at a constant rate of about **one drink per hour**.

Factors That Affect a Guest's BAC

How high and how quickly a guest's BAC rises depends on several factors, including:

- **Rate of consumption and amount consumed.** As alcohol moves through the body, the effect it has on a guest's BAC depends on the rate at which it enters the bloodstream. Since the liver can remove alcohol from the body at the rate of only one drink per hour, consuming more will result in a buildup in the guest's bloodstream, raising his or her BAC.

  Let's say a customer orders two drinks in an hour. While the liver is breaking down the alcohol in the first drink, the alcohol in the second drink gets backed up and stays in the bloodstream. What if the customer orders three more drinks in the next hour? While the alcohol in the second drink is being broken down, there are now three drinks backed up in the bloodstream.

  Alcohol can affect guests long after they have stopped drinking. Although they may appear fine, guests may become intoxicated after leaving the establishment, since alcohol will continue to enter their bloodstreams.

- **Drink strength.** The more alcohol a drink contains, the more that will end up in the bloodstream and the higher the BAC. Distilled liquor, such as whiskey or vodka, contains a larger percentage of alcohol by volume than does fermented liquor such as beer or wine. A person drinking a two-ounce martini will have a higher BAC than a person drinking a 12-ounce beer, all other factors being the same.

Higher BAC Lower BAC

- **Body type.** A guest's size and percentage of body fat will affect his or her BAC.
  - **Body size.** Drink for drink, a small person will have a higher BAC than a large person because the small person has less blood in his or her body to dilute the alcohol.

  - **Body fat.** A person with a large percentage of body fat will have a higher BAC than a lean person if both drink the same amount of alcohol. Body fat does not absorb alcohol, forcing it to remain in the bloodstream until broken down by the liver. However, alcohol can pass through muscle in a lean person and spread throughout the entire body.

Higher BAC

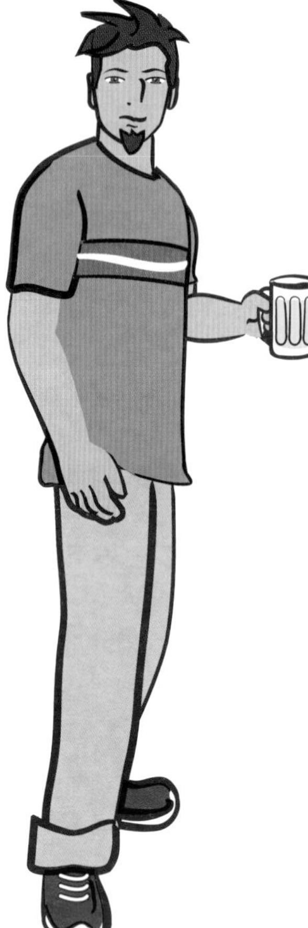

Lower BAC

Higher BAC Lower BAC

- **Gender.** Drink for drink, a woman will have a higher BAC than a man if both are of equal size. Women have a higher percentage of body fat and a smaller amount of a stomach enzyme that helps break down alcohol. They are also typically smaller than men, and therefore have less blood in their bodies.

- **Age.** A senior citizen who drinks the same amount of alcohol as a younger guest will have a higher BAC—all other factors being the same. Body fat typically increases with age, and enzyme action tends to slow down as a person gets older.

Higher BAC Lower BAC

- **Emotional state.** An emotional guest will have a higher BAC than a guest who is calm, all other factors being the same. When a person is stressed, angry, or afraid, the body diverts blood away from the stomach and small intestine to the muscles. This reduced blood flow slows the absorption of alcohol into the bloodstream. The guest will not feel the effects of the alcohol, and may continue to drink. As he or she begins to calm and blood flow returns to the stomach, the guest may experience a sudden increase in his or her BAC.

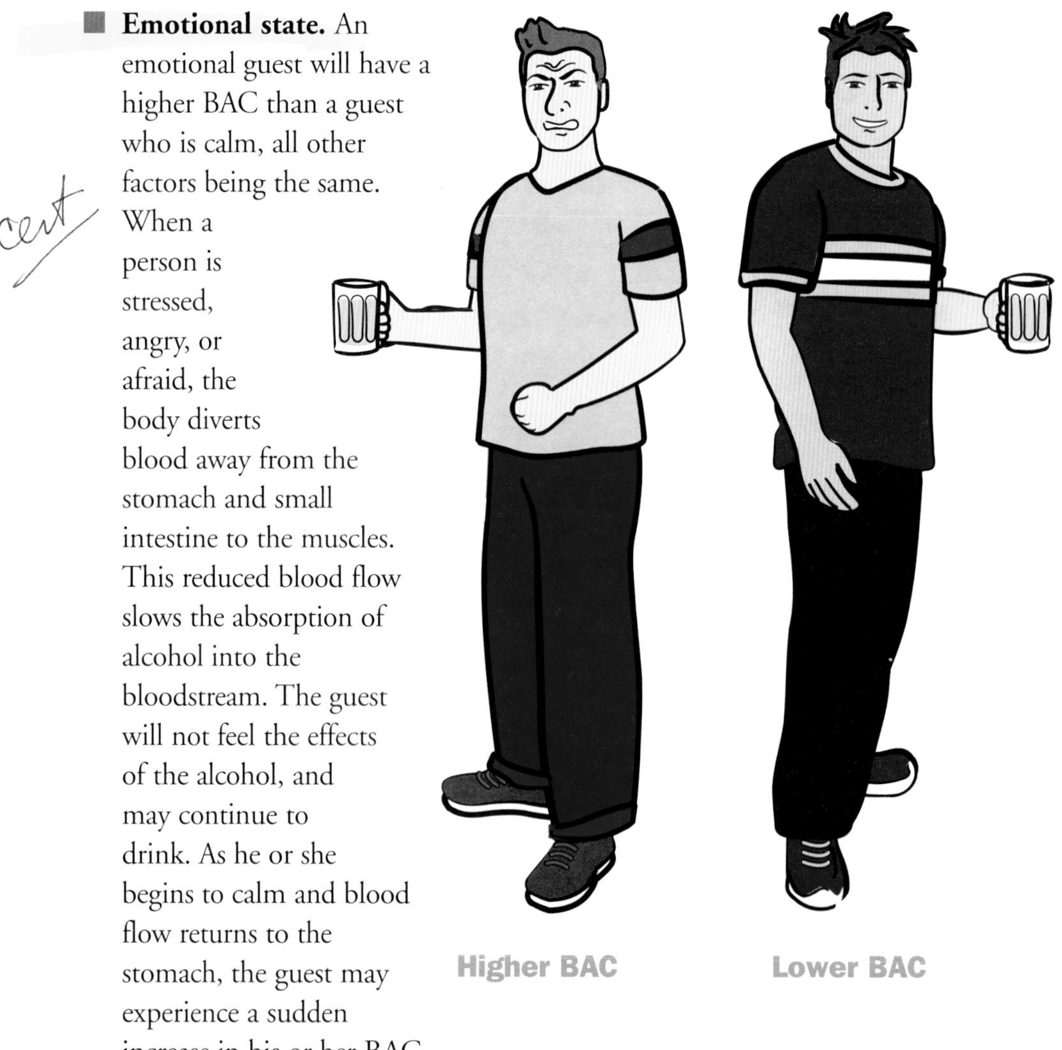

- **Medications.** Guests who consume alcohol while using illegal drugs or medications—such as cold tablets, tranquilizers, antihistamines, or high blood pressure medications, can compound the effects of alcohol or expose themselves to dangerous interactions.

  It is often difficult to know if a guest is taking medication. Sometimes, you may notice signs of illness such as coughing, sneezing, runny nose, etc. This may be a good opportunity to ask the guest how he or she is feeling and to find out if the individual is taking medication.

- **Food.** A guest who has not eaten will have a higher BAC than a guest who has eaten, all other factors being the same. One of the major factors impacting the rate that alcohol enters the bloodstream is food. Food keeps alcohol in the stomach for a longer period of time, slowing the rate at which it reaches the small intestine.

  Take special care if you know a guest is dieting, since the individual may not have eaten or may have eaten considerably less than usual. Alcohol may pass more quickly from his or her stomach to the small intestine.

Higher BAC Lower BAC

Higher BAC Lower BAC

- **Carbonation.** A guest who is drinking a carbonated drink, such as sparkling wine or vodka and tonic, will have a higher BAC than a guest who is drinking an alcoholic beverage without carbonation, all other factors being the same. Carbonation may speed the rate at which alcohol passes through the stomach, causing a person to reach a higher BAC at a faster rate.

Keep in mind that some guests will have a combination of these factors, resulting in a higher risk of intoxication. For example, an elderly woman on medication who is consuming a martini, or an obviously irritated man with a high percentage of body fat who has had two Long Island ice teas in an hour, are both at higher risks for intoxication. These types of guests require even more attention on your part to prevent intoxication.

APPLY YOUR KNOWLEDGE: *Whose BAC is Higher?*

Assuming that each pair of guests is consuming drinks at the same rate, which guest will more likely have a higher BAC? Explain your choice in the space provided.

1. ______________________________

2. ______________________________

3. ______________________________

Continued on next page...

Guest 1 Guest 2

4. ______________________________

Guest 1 Guest 2

5. ______________________________

For answers, please turn to page 2-30.

ASSESSING A GUEST'S LEVEL OF INTOXICATION

To prevent overservice, you must be able to properly assess a guest's level of intoxication. There are two ways to do this:

1. **Count the number of drinks you serve.**
2. **Observe behavior.**

Using a combination of the two is the best approach for preventing guests from becoming intoxicated.

Counting Drinks

Counting drinks is a useful tool for determining whether or not a guest is intoxicated. To accurately count drinks, however, you need to know how much alcohol they contain.

Proof is a measure of a liquor's strength, or the percentage of alcohol it contains. The percentage is determined by dividing the liquor's proof by two. For example, 100-proof whiskey is 50 percent alcohol (100 ÷ 2 = 50), while 80-proof vodka is 40 percent alcohol. Thus, the whiskey is stronger because it contains more alcohol.

The following beverages serve as the standard measure when counting drinks. They contain approximately the same amount of pure alcohol (half ounce), and should be counted as one drink.

Here is another way to look at these standard measures when counting drinks:

DISTILLED LIQUOR	
PROOF	**AMOUNT IN ONE DRINK**
100	1 ounce
80	1.5 ounces
40	2.5 ounces

FERMENTED LIQUOR	
TYPE	**AMOUNT IN ONE DRINK**
Beer	12 ounces
Wine	5 ounces

Whether a liquor is served straight, such as a one-ounce shot of 80-proof vodka, or diluted in a mixed drink, such as a vodka and tonic containing one ounce of 80-proof vodka, the alcohol content is the same. Adding a nonalcoholic beverage (mixer) to a drink does not alter the alcohol content.

It is also important to note that some beers, flavored malt beverages, and wines have a higher alcohol content, and therefore must be counted differently than the standard beverages listed on the previous page.

Other factors that affect the way a drink is counted include:

- **Size of the drink.** Some beverages contain more than a single serving of liquor. To find the actual number of drinks in these cocktails, divide the liquor in the cocktail by the standard amount of that liquor found in one drink. (See the tables on page 2-12 for a review of standard measures.)

For example, a dry gin martini containing three ounces of 80-proof gin would be counted as two drinks since:

3	÷	1.5	=	2
ounces of 80-proof gin		ounces of 80-proof gin in 1 drink		Total number of drinks

Martini

Here's another example. You now know that a 12-ounce beer is counted as one drink, but how many drinks are contained in a 24-ounce beer? The answer is two. Here's why:

24	÷	12	=	2
ounces of beer		ounces of beer in 1 drink		Total number of drinks

24-ounce Beer

- **Contents of the drink.** Mixed drinks may contain liquors with different proofs. Some contain cordials and liqueurs, which may be as little as 20-percent alcohol, or 40-proof.

  Counting drinks containing multiple liquors can be challenging, especially if those liquors have different proofs. For example, the Long Island ice tea below contains three 80-proof liquors (one ounce each of vodka, gin, and rum) and one 40-proof liquor (one ounce of triple sec). To determine the number of drinks in this cocktail, you must calculate the number of drinks for each liquor, and then add the totals together. According to the recipe, the Long Island ice tea would be counted as 2.5 drinks. Here's why:

Long Island ice tea

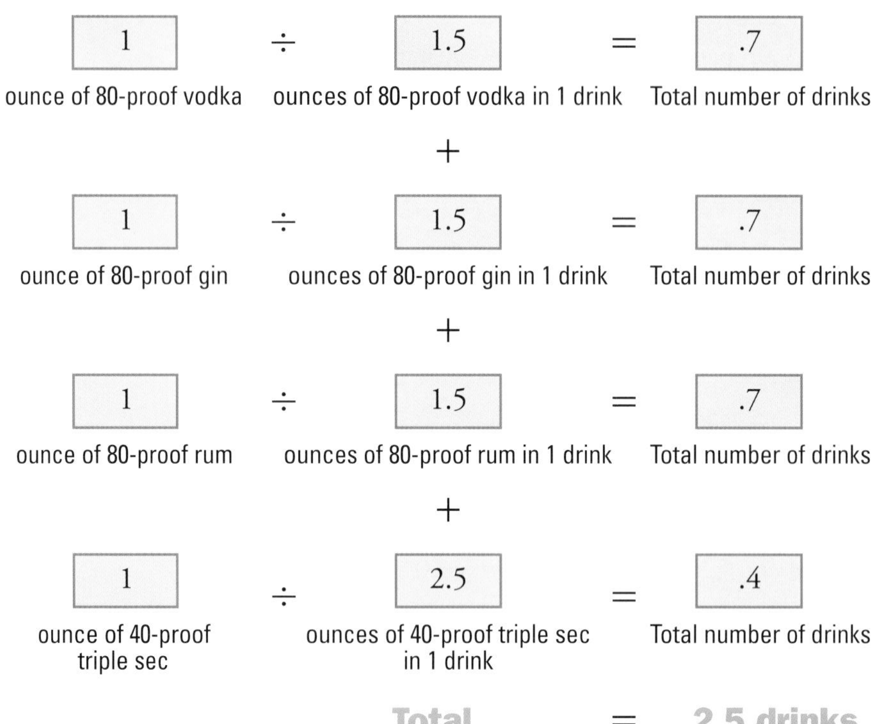

Take a look at the alcoholic beverages served in your establishment, and calculate the number of drinks in each one. (Your manager might already have done this for you.) This information will be important for accurately counting the drinks consumed by your guests.

APPLY YOUR KNOWLEDGE: *Count the Drinks*

Calculate the number of drinks in each item and write the number in the space provided.

1. 5.3 64-ounce pitcher of beer
2. 2 3 ounces of 80-proof vodka on the rocks
3. 1.7 Margarita containing 2 ounces of 80-proof tequila and 1 ounce of 40-proof triple sec
4. 1.6 8-ounce glass of wine
5. 1.3 16-ounce glass of beer

For answers, please turn to page 2-30.

Calculating BAC

If you count the number of drinks consumed by your guests and can estimate their approximate weight, you can get a rough idea of their BAC using the charts on the next page. Each chart is based on one hour of drinking, accounting for the liver breaking down alcohol at a rate of one drink per hour.

How many drinks can a guest safely consume? How much is too much? As you know, a BAC of .08 is the legal level of intoxication while driving in the U.S. The values in the charts highlighted in red indicate a BAC of .08 or higher. While you are not legally responsible for knowing your guest's BAC, counting drinks and using these charts—along with watching for visible signs of intoxication (which you will learn about in the next section)—will help you make the best decisions while serving.

These charts should be used only as a reference. A guest's actual BAC may be higher or lower since the chart cannot account for other factors, such as prior drinking, the guest's physical condition, emotional state, and/or consumption of food or medication. Also, guests may exhibit signs of intoxication at a lower BAC.

Blood Alcohol Content (BAC) Estimation Charts

MEN

(after one hour of drinking)

Body Weight

Number of Drinks	100	120	140	160	180	200	220	240
1	.022	.015	.011	.007	.005	.003	.001	.000
2	.059	.046	.038	.031	.026	.022	.018	.015
3	.097	.078	.064	.054	.046	.040	.035	.031
4	.134	.109	.091	.078	.067	.059	.052	.046
5	.172	.140	.118	.101	.088	.078	.069	.062
6	.209	.172	.145	.125	.109	.097	.086	.078
7	.247	.203	.172	.148	.130	.115	.103	.093
8	.284	.234	.198	.172	.151	.134	.120	.109

Indicates a BAC of .08 or higher

Markham, M.R., Miller, W.R. & Arciniega, L. (1993) BACCuS 2.01: Computer software for quantifying alcohol consumption. Behavior Research Methods, Instruments, & Computers, 25, 420-421

WOMEN

(after one hour of drinking)

Body Weight

Number of Drinks	100	120	140	160	180	200	220	240
1	.029	.022	.016	.012	.009	.006	.004	.003
2	.074	.059	.048	.040	.034	.029	.025	.022
3	.119	.097	.080	.068	.059	.052	.045	.040
4	.164	.134	.113	.096	.084	.074	.066	.059
5	.209	.172	.145	.125	.109	.097	.086	.078
6	.254	.209	.177	.153	134	.119	.107	.097
7	.299	.247	.209	.181	.159	.142	.127	.115
8	.344	.284	.241	.209	.184	.164	.148	.134

Indicates a BAC of .08 or higher

Markham, M.R., Miller, W.R. & Arciniega, L. (1993) BACCuS 2.01: Computer software for quantifying alcohol consumption. Behavior Research Methods, Instruments, & Computers, 25, 420-421

Let's say that a 120-pound woman has consumed two drinks in an hour. Using the chart for women, her approximate BAC would be .059. On the other hand, it would take four drinks for a 200-pound man to reach the same BAC.

APPLY YOUR KNOWLEDGE: *What Are Their BACs?*

Estimate the BAC of each guest using the charts on page 2-16 and write it in the space provided.

1. ______ 160-pound man who has consumed five 12-ounce beers in one hour
2. ______ 100-pound woman who has consumed three 5-ounce glasses of wine in one hour
3. ______ 120-pound man who has consumed two vodka on the rocks, each containing 3 ounces of 80-proof vodka, in one hour
4. ______ 240-pound man who has consumed two shots (two ounces) of 100-proof bourbon and two 12-ounce beers in one hour
5. ______ 140-pound woman who has consumed two strawberry daiquiris, each containing 3 ounces of 80-proof rum, in one hour

For answers, please turn to page 2-30.

When to Count Drinks

You should start counting drinks when guests place their first order, and continue counting until they leave the premises. There are many ways to do this. In bar areas, a tab can be left in front of the guest so bartenders and servers can monitor it. For dining guests, servers can keep a drink tally on the back of the guest check. In some establishments, the guest check moves with the guest, which makes counting easier.

Bar tabs can help bartenders and servers count drinks.

In some situations, counting drinks can be difficult, if not impossible. For example, servers at banquets have unique problems when attempting to count drinks because guests move around and may be served at different locations. If counting drinks will not work, you must rely on observation to spot signs of intoxication.

HOW THIS RELATES TO ME...

What is your company policy regarding counting drinks? List some ways that you count drinks in your establishment.

Observing Guests for Signs of Intoxication

In addition to counting drinks, you can learn a lot about how the alcohol your guests have consumed is affecting them by carefully watching for physical and behavioral changes. Keep in mind that a change in behavior is more significant than the actual behavior itself. There is a big difference between a normally loud and boisterous guest and a guest who is quiet when he or she first arrives at your establishment and then becomes loud and boisterous after a few drinks. Communication is also important. Taking the time to talk to your guests in addition to observing their behavior will help you determine the purpose of their visit as well as their level of intoxication. If guests are determined to become intoxicated, you want to know about it. Continue talking to each guest throughout his or her stay.

Watching for changes and talking to your guests can also help prevent a potentially embarrassing situation. Certain disabilities and physical conditions can cause a guest to stumble, slur his or her speech, or have difficulty concentrating. Observation and communication will help you avoid mistakenly seeing these actions as signs of intoxication.

Physical and Behavioral Signs of Intoxication

When large amounts of alcohol reach the brain, it can no longer function normally. This results in physical and behavioral changes, including relaxed inhibitions, impaired judgment, slowed reaction time, and impaired motor coordination.

- **Relaxed inhibitions.** Inhibitions restrain or suppress a person's emotions, actions, or thoughts. A guest's normal inhibitions will become relaxed, allowing the person to say or do things he or she normally would not. Guests with relaxed inhibitions may
  - be overly friendly.
  - be unfriendly, depressed, or quiet.
  - use foul language.
  - become loud.
  - make rude comments.
- **Impaired judgment.** A guest's ability to make sensible decisions will be affected. Guests with impaired judgment may
  - complain about the strength of a drink after having consumed others of the same strength.
  - begin drinking faster or switch to larger or stronger drinks.
  - make irrational or argumentative statements.
  - become careless with money (i.e., buying drinks for strangers).
- **Slowed reaction time.** A guest's reaction time and responses will become slower. Guests with slowed reaction time may
  - talk or move slowly.
  - be unable to concentrate, lose their train of thought, or become forgetful.
  - become drowsy.
  - become glassy eyed, lose eye contact, or become unable to focus.

Guests with relaxed inhibitions may be overly friendly.

Guests with impaired judgment may become careless with money and buy drinks for strangers.

Guests with slowed reaction time will often become drowsy or fall asleep.

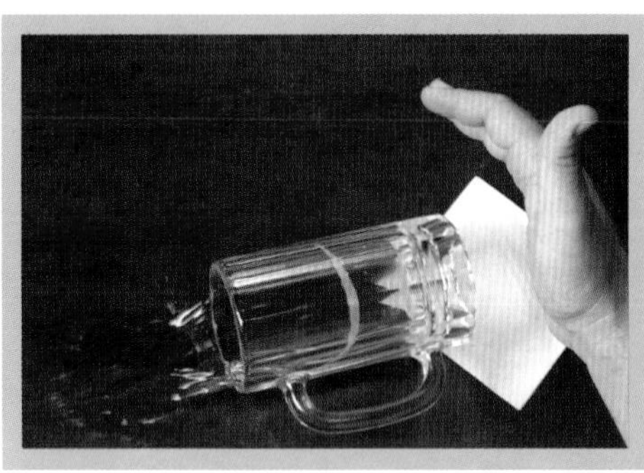

Guests with impaired motor coordination may spill drinks.

- **Impaired motor coordination.** A guest's motor skills will be affected. Guests with impaired motor coordination may
  - stagger, stumble, fall down, or bump into objects.
  - be unable to pick up objects, or may drop them.
  - spill drinks or miss their mouths when drinking.
  - sway when sitting or standing.
  - slur their speech.
  - have difficulty lighting a cigarette.

Tolerance to Alcohol

People can build up a tolerance to alcohol. Tolerance is the ability to endure the effects of alcohol without exhibiting the usual signs. An experienced drinker can often consume a lot of alcohol without showing its effects. These individuals have learned to hide them—even after becoming intoxicated. This makes it difficult for you to assess this type of guest by observation alone. Remember: tolerance does not affect a guest's BAC, just his or her ability to hide the effects of alcohol.

Regulars

Most establishments have guests who are regular patrons. As a server, you can become used to the drinking habits of these regulars and their ability to handle their liquor. They may be leaving your establishment, however, with a dangerously high BAC. In fact, the majority of alcohol-related incidents involve regular patrons. Use your knowledge of alcohol's effects on the body—and count drinks.

Inexperienced Drinkers

Another type of guest who should be closely monitored is the inexperienced drinker. These guests often show signs of intoxication after drinking a small amount of alcohol because their bodies are unaccustomed to it and sensitive to smaller amounts. Remember: while guests may have had only one or two drinks at your establishment, you can be held liable if they were visibly intoxicated when they left.

SOMETHING TO THINK ABOUT...

Steve was a regular patron at Half Time Bar and Grill, which he visited at least three times a week. Everyone knew Steve and liked him. Kelly—on her first day on the job—served him a small salad and five beers in the course of an hour. She noticed that Steve was more relaxed but otherwise seemed fine. Kelly was amazed at Steve's tolerance.

Later, she said to Mary, a more experienced server, "Man, he can sure drink a lot." Mary replied, "Yeah, he's been coming here for years. He's fine. He must have a liver of steel." While Kelly was concerned about how much Steve had been drinking, she overlooked it after talking to Mary.

After three hours and eleven beers, Steve left the restaurant. The next morning, the manager on duty received a call from the local police. The previous evening, Steve was in a car accident and had killed the mother of two children and injured himself. He had a BAC of .21 at the time of the accident.

How do you think Kelly, who overserved Steve, feels?

The Importance of Observation and Communication

Monitor guests from the moment they arrive on the premises until they are ready to leave. When a guest shows signs of intoxication, that information must be communicated to management and the appropriate coworkers. If guests move from the bar to another location, such as a table in the dining room, information about the amount of alcohol they have consumed should go with them. To be successful when evaluating guests, you will need input from coworkers who have come in contact with them. This includes:

- Valets
- Waitstaff
- Bus staff
- Bartenders
- Security, hosts, hostesses and greeters
- Coat check and restroom attendants

Valets can spot signs of intoxication by watching guests get out of their car.

Valets

Valets often are the first people to make contact with guests. If you are a valet, you should identify intoxicated guests and alert your manager before they enter the establishment and attempt to be served.

As you observe guests, ask yourself the following questions:

- Is their driving erratic?
- Are they having difficulty parking between the lines in the parking space?
- Are they having difficulty getting out of the car or walking?
- Are they having difficulty talking?
- Do you smell alcohol?

If you can answer *Yes* to any one of these questions, there may be cause for concern and you should notify your manager. If you suspect a guest is intoxicated, never ask him or her to leave the premises in that condition. You should take steps to keep that person from leaving in that condition. (Handling this type of situation will be addressed in Chapter 4.)

Hosts and hostesses should talk to guests to look for signs of intoxication.

Security, Hosts and Hostesses, and Greeters

Security staff, hosts and hostesses, and/or greeters often are the first people to make contact with guests once they have stepped inside the establishment. Use your greeting as an opportunity to talk to the guests and to observe the following:

- Are they speaking rationally?
- Is their speech slurred?
- Are they able to make eye contact and focus while talking to you?
- Can they walk without staggering, stumbling, or bumping into objects?

Bus Staff

Bus staff are in a unique position to observe guest behavior. If you are bussing tables, use the opportunity to listen to how guests speak and to observe the following:

- Are they getting louder as time passes?
- Are they becoming overfriendly, or are they beginning to use foul language or becoming rude?
- Have they started spilling drinks or food on the table?
- Are they having difficulty talking?
- Are they beginning to look tired or sleepy?

If you notice any of these behaviors, talk to your manager.

Bus staff can spot signs of intoxication by observing and listening to guests.

HOW THIS RELATES TO ME...

How do you communicate information about intoxicated guests in your establishment?

APPLY YOUR KNOWLEDGE: *Rate the Guest*

This activity requires Video/DVD 5: *Evaluating Real-World Scenarios.* After watching each scenario from Section 1 of this video/DVD, use the rating scale below to rate whether or not the guest(s) are intoxicated by placing the appropriate number in the space provided.

Rating Scale
1 = Guest is not intoxicated (is sober).
2 = Guest is intoxicated.

Video Segment	Description	Rating
1	Valet interacting with a guest leaving the establishment	
2	Two female guests eating in a fine-dining restaurant	
3	Senior citizen sitting at a table	
4	Guest talking to a female server at the end of the bar	
5	Two male guests watching a football game at a bar	
6	Female guest talking with a bartender at the bar	
7	Male and female guests drinking in a nightclub	
8	Male guest entering an establishment	
9	Construction worker drinking at the bar	
10	Regular interacting with a bartender at the bar	

For answers, please turn to page 2-31.

PREVENTING GUESTS FROM BECOMING INTOXICATED

As a seller or server of alcohol, you must do everything possible to ensure that guests do not become intoxicated at your establishment. This can sometimes be a difficult task, but there are some simple things you can do. These practices will help guests drink responsibly—they are also hallmarks of good service.

- **Offer food.** Offering food is one of the most important things you can do to help prevent intoxication. Remember: food helps keep alcohol in the stomach, slowing the rate at which it reaches the small intestine. Some types of food do a better job than others. **Food high in fat and/or protein, such as pizza, chicken wings, cheese, and deep-fried items, is the best type to serve because it is digested more slowly. *Avoid* serving food items that are:**
  - **High in sugar or carbohydrates**—While better than nothing, these items are easily digested and thus less effective in slowing the movement of alcohol into the small intestine.
  - **Salty**—While food such as peanuts, pretzels, and chips is common bar fare, these items can make guests thirsty and increase their consumption of alcohol.

Deep-fried items are one of the best types of food to serve with alcohol.

- **Offer water.** Drinking alcohol causes dehydration, making guests thirsty. This can cause them to drink more than they ordinarily would to quench their thirst. You can help by offering water with drinks and refilling water glasses often.
- **Avoid overpouring when mixing drinks.** Overpouring makes it difficult to count the actual number of drinks consumed by a guest. It also makes it difficult for guests to keep track of, and regulate, their own drinking. For example, let's say that the recipe for a gin and tonic calls for one-and-a-half ounces of 80-proof gin. If you mix three gin and tonics for a guest, but you overpour the gin in each drink by a half ounce, you have actually served the guest four drinks instead of three! Follow house recipes and be consistent. Guests should not be able to tell when different bartenders are making their drinks.
- **Avoid serving the guest more than one drink at a time.** This will help pace the guest's consumption.

Offer water with drinks.

out

APPLY YOUR KNOWLEDGE: *Which Food Is Best?*

Place an X in front of the food items that are best for preventing intoxication.

1. ____ Bread
2. ____ Pizza
3. ____ Potato chips
4. ____ Cheese sticks
5. ____ Chili
6. ____Onion rings
7. ____Pretzels
8. ____Peanuts
9. ____Fried calamari
10. ____Chicken wings

For answers, please turn to page 2-32.

HOW THIS RELATES TO ME...

List the types of appetizers served in your establishment that can help prevent intoxication.

____

____

____

SUMMARY

When a person drinks alcohol, the majority of it is absorbed into the bloodstream through the small intestine. Once in the bloodstream, alcohol travels quickly throughout the body, reaching the brain in minutes. Only the liver can break down alcohol, which it does at a constant rate of about one drink per hour. Consuming more than this will result in a buildup of alcohol in the bloodstream.

How quickly and how high a guest's BAC rises depends on several factors, including the rate of consumption, drink strength, and amount consumed. Body type, gender, age, and the guest's emotional state play factors, as does the amount of food consumed and whether or not a drink is carbonated.

There are two ways to assess a guest's level of intoxication—counting the number of drinks served and/or observing the guest for physical and behavioral changes. A combination of these two approaches is best for preventing intoxication. In order to accurately count drinks, you need to know how much alcohol they contain. The following alcoholic beverages contain approximately the same amount of alcohol and should be counted as one drink: a 12-ounce beer, a five-ounce glass of wine, one-and-a-half ounces of 80-proof liquor, and one ounce of 100-proof liquor.

While these beverages serve as the standard measure when counting drinks, some will be counted differently. The proof of the liquor used and the serving size of the drink will affect the count. If you can identify a guest's approximate weight and have counted the number of drinks he or she has consumed, you can get a rough estimate of the person's BAC using a blood alcohol content estimation chart. These charts should be used only as a general reference.

In addition to counting drinks, you can learn a lot about a guest's level of intoxication by carefully watching for physical and behavioral changes. Keep in mind that a change in behavior is more significant than the actual behavior itself. When large amounts of alcohol reach the brain, it can no longer function normally. This results in physical and behavioral changes, including relaxed inhibitions, impaired judgment, slowed reaction time, and impaired motor coordination.

Tolerance is the ability to endure the effects of alcohol without exhibiting the usual signs of intoxication. An experienced drinker can often consume a large quantity of alcohol without showing its effects. These individuals have learned to hide the effects—even after becoming intoxicated. You must be careful when dealing with regular drinkers at your establishment who may have a high tolerance. They may be leaving with a dangerously high BAC. Use your knowledge of alcohol's effect on the body—and count drinks.

As a seller or server of alcohol, there are several things you can do to prevent a guest from becoming intoxicated. One of the most important is offering food. Remember: food keeps alcohol in the stomach for a longer period of time, slowing the rate at which it reaches the small intestine. The best food items are fatty and high in protein, since these types of food are digested more slowly. It is also important to offer water to guests, as they will become dehydrated while drinking alcohol. Avoid overpouring when mixing drinks. Overpouring makes it difficult to count the actual number of drinks consumed by a guest. Follow house recipes when mixing drinks, and be consistent. Finally, avoid serving guests more than one drink at a time.

MULTIPLE-CHOICE STUDY QUESTIONS

?

1. **Most of the alcohol a person consumes is absorbed into the bloodstream from the**
   A. lungs.
   B. mouth.
   C. small intestine.
   D. liver.

2. **The liver can break down alcohol at the rate of ___ drink(s) per hour.**
   A. one
   B. two
   C. three
   D. four

3. **A guest has consumed three 12-ounce beers in an hour. How many drinks are still backed up in his bloodstream?**
   A. None
   B. One
   C. Two
   D. Three

4. **Assuming that they weigh the same and have consumed the same number of drinks, which of the following statements is true?**
   A. A man will have a higher BAC than a woman.
   B. A lean man will have a higher BAC than a man with a large amount of body fat.
   C. A woman who has eaten will have a higher BAC than a woman who has not.
   D. A man drinking gin and tonic will have a higher BAC than a man drinking vodka and cranberry juice.

5. **All of the following alcoholic beverages should be counted as one drink *except***
   A. a 12-ounce beer.
   B. a five-ounce glass of wine.
   C. two ounces of 80-proof liquor.
   D. one ounce of 100-proof liquor.

Continued on next page...

MULTIPLE-CHOICE STUDY QUESTIONS
continued

?

6. **A margarita containing three ounces of 80-proof tequila and one-and-a-half ounces of 40-proof triple sec should be counted as approximately ___ drink(s).**
   A. one
   B. two and a half
   C. three and a half
   D. four

7. **Which of the following behaviors is a sign that a guest is experiencing relaxed inhibitions?**
   A. He is becoming loud.
   B. He is slurring his speech.
   C. He is having difficulty making eye contact.
   D. He is drinking faster and switching to stronger drinks.

8. **Which of the following behaviors is a sign that a guest is experiencing impaired motor coordination?**
   A. She is becoming drowsy.
   B. She is having difficulty lighting her cigarette.
   C. She is making rude comments.
   D. She is having trouble concentrating.

9. **What is the best type of food to help prevent intoxication?**
   A. Salty food
   B. Carbohydrates
   C. Sugars
   D. Proteins

10. **All of the following can help prevent a guest from becoming intoxicated *except***
   A. serving water.
   B. serving one drink at a time.
   C. being consistent when pouring drinks.
   D. offering a guest approaching intoxication a beer instead of a martini.

For answers, please turn to page 2-32.

ANSWERS

Page	Activity
2-2	**Test Your Knowledge** 1. False 2. False 3. False 4. False 5. True
2-4	**Believe It or Not?** None of these activities removes a large amount of alcohol from the body.

2-10 Whose BAC Is Higher?

1. Guest 1 will probably have a higher BAC. She has a higher percentage of body fat, which will force the alcohol she consumes to remain in the bloodstream until broken down by the liver. Guest 2, on the other hand, is lean, which means that the alcohol she consumes can pass from her bloodstream through her muscles and spread throughout her body. Guest 1 is also visibly angry. Since blood flow is being diverted away from her small intestine, she may drink more because she might not be feeling the effects of alcohol. As she begins to calm and blood flow returns, she may experience a sudden increase in her BAC.
2. Guest 2 will probably have a higher BAC. Although they are similar in size, the woman would have a higher percentage of body fat and a smaller amount of a stomach enzyme that helps to break down alcohol. Therefore, she would have a higher BAC. Also, she is drinking a martini. Compared to Guest 1's glass of wine, the martini contains more alcohol, so more of it will end up in her bloodstream.
3. Guest 2 will probably have a higher BAC. Guest 2 is a senior citizen whose enzyme actions may have slowed with age. Guest 1 is much younger. A senior citizen who drinks the same amount of alcohol as a younger guest will have a higher BAC, all other factors being the same.
4. Guest 2 will probably have a higher BAC. Guest 2 is smaller than Guest 1, which means that she has less blood in her body to dilute the alcohol that she has consumed. Also, Guest 2 is drinking champagne—a carbonated beverage. Carbonation may cause the alcohol to pass into the bloodstream more quickly.
5. Guest 1 will probably have a higher BAC. A guest's BAC depends upon the quantity of alcohol entering the bloodstream. Guest 1 is drinking a larger amount of beer (24 ounces) and is not eating. Since he is not eating, the alcohol he is drinking may pass more quickly from his stomach to his small intestine. On the other hand, Guest 2 is drinking a smaller beer (12 ounces) and is also eating. Food keeps alcohol in the stomach for a longer period of time, slowing the rate at which it reaches the small intestine.

2-15 Count the Drinks

1. 5.3 2. 2 3. 1.7 4. 1.6 5. 1.3

2-17 What's Are Their BACs?

1. This man has had five drinks, since a 12-ounce beer is considered one drink. His approximate BAC would be .101.
2. This woman has had three drinks, since a five-ounce glass of wine is considered one drink. Her approximate BAC is .119.
3. This man actually had four drinks. He consumed six ounces of vodka (one-and-a-half ounces of 80-proof liquor equals one drink). His approximate BAC is .109.
4. This man actually had four drinks, since each 100-proof shot is considered one drink. His approximate BAC would be .046.
5. This woman actually had four drinks, since she consumed six ounces of 80-proof liquor. Her approximate BAC would be .113.

Continued on next page...

ANSWERS continued

Page Activity

2-24 Rate the Guest

1. Rating: 2—Intoxicated.

   Indicators of intoxication:

   - The guest was staggering and swaying.
   - The guest spilled money from his pocket on the ground and had difficulty picking it up.
   - The guest was loud.
   - The guest had impaired speech.

2. Rating: 2—Intoxicated.

   Indicators of intoxication:

   - The guest repeatedly spilled wine.
   - The guests were inappropriately loud.
   - The guest's speech was impaired (had difficulty choosing her words).

3. Rating: 1—Sober.

   Indicators of sobriety:

   - At this point, the guest was not showing any signs of intoxication. The fact that he had taken medication, however, should have alerted the server that he is at risk for intoxication.
   - The fact that the guest ordered a double should also be of concern to the server.

4. Rating: 2—Intoxicated.

   Indicators of intoxication:

   - The guest was overly friendly.
   - The guest made rude comments.
   - The guest's speech was impaired.

5. Rating: 1—Sober.

   Indicators of sobriety:

   - The guests were speaking clearly (no sign of slurring).
   - The guests were eating fatty food, which slows the absorption of alcohol.
   - The guests used good judgment and had a single beer each rather than ordering another pitcher.

6. Rating: 2—Intoxicated.

   Indicators of intoxication:

   - The guest complained about the strength of her drinks.
   - The guest became argumentative.

7. Rating: 2—Intoxicated.

   Indicators of intoxication:

   - The man and the woman became too intimate for people who didn't know each other.

Continued on next page...

ANSWERS continued

Page Activity

8. Rating: 2—Intoxicated.
   Indicators of intoxication:
   - The guest used profanity.
   - The guest bumped into obstacles in his path.
   - The guest was loud and unfriendly.
9. Rating: 1—Sober.
   Indicators of sobriety:
   - While the guest ordered four drinks (three shots of 100-proof bourbon and a 12-ounce beer), he only consumed about three-and-a-half drinks, since his beer was still half full. Since the guest was clearly over 200 pounds, muscular, and had most likely consumed food, he was not intoxicated.
   - While the guest's rate of consumption could have caused concern, it was not an issue at the time.
10. Rating: 2—Intoxicated.
    Indicators of intoxication:
    - While the guest was not exhibiting any physical or behavioral signs of intoxication, he probably was intoxicated based on his size and drink count. He consumed four martinis, which, depending on the recipe, may be counted as six to eight drinks.
    - The guest had a high tolerance to alcohol.

2-26 Which Food Is Best?

1. No. Bread is a carbohydrate, which is easily digested.
2. Yes. The cheese on pizza makes it a fatty food, which is digested more slowly.
3. No. While potato chips are fried, they are carbohydrates and are salty, making them a poor choice.
4. Yes. Cheese is a fatty food. It is also deep-fried, making it a good choice.
5. Yes. The meat in the chili is a protein, which is digested more slowly.
6. Yes. The deep-fried onion rings are fatty, and are therefore digested more slowly.
7. No. Pretzels are carbohydrates, which are digested quickly. They are also salty, which can cause thirst and increase the consumption of alcohol.
8. No. The peanuts are not really a good choice since they are salty, which can cause thirst and increase the consumption of alcohol.
9. Yes. Deep-fried calamari contains protein and it is a fatty food, which is digested more slowly.
10. Yes. The chicken is a protein, which takes time to digest. The chicken also has been deep-fried, making it a good choice.

2-28 Multiple-Choice Study Questions

1. C
2. A
3. C
4. D
5. C
6. B
7. A
8. B
9. D
10. D

NOTES

3 Checking Identification

After completing this chapter, you should be able to:

- Identify acceptable forms of identification.
- Identify the characteristics of a valid ID.
- Identify valid IDs issued to minors.
- Verify that an ID is genuine.
- Verify that an ID belongs to the guest who has presented it.
- Identify when to check IDs.
- Identify the proper procedure for checking IDs.
- Properly use bar-code and magnetic-stripe ID readers.
- Identify the proper way to deal with a fake ID.

TEST YOUR KNOWLEDGE

1. **True or False:** A birth certificate is an acceptable form of identification. *(See page 3-5.)*
2. **True or False:** To be valid, an ID must contain a state seal. *(See page 3-5.)*
3. **True or False:** An ID with split lamination is not valid. *(See page 3-5.)*
4. **True or False:** IDs containing the words "Official," "Authentic," or "Secure" are not genuine. *(See page 3-10.)*
5. **True or False:** A guest that avoids eye contact while you are carding him may have presented a fake or altered ID. *(See page 3-14.)*

For answers, please turn to page 3-20.

CONCEPTS

- **Hologram:** Three-dimensional image that appears to change when viewed from different angles.
- **Lamination:** Plastic film enclosing many state-issued IDs.
- **Ghost photo image:** Faint copy of the photo added to the ID as a security feature.
- **ID checking guide:** Reference used to validate IDs. It includes samples of each state's drivers' licenses and a detailed description of minor IDs, state ID cards, and valid drivers' licenses in current circulation.
- **ID reader:** Device used to validate IDs by reading information encoded in an ID's bar codes or magnetic stripes.

APPLY YOUR KNOWLEDGE: *Spot the Minor*

Which of these people is a minor?

For answers, please turn to page 3-20.

INTRODUCTION

While all of the women in the photos look at least 21 years of age, all of them are minors. The woman in photo #1 is only 17-years old!

Many minors today look much older than they actually are. For this reason, it is dangerous to make a decision about service on a guess or hunch about a guest's age. As a seller or server of alcohol, you are responsible for ensuring that all of your guests are of legal age to drink. This can be a challenging task given the fast-paced environment in which you work. If there is any doubt about a guest's age, however, you must take the appropriate steps to verify that he or she is of legal age to drink. You have the legal right to refuse service if you suspect the guest is underage. Remember: you can be held criminally liable for serving a minor.

ACCEPTABLE FORMS OF IDENTIFICATION

The types of identification that can be used to confirm a guest's age depends upon what is legally acceptable in your state or municipality. In most states, the following forms of ID are acceptable:

Driver's License

State ID Card

Military ID

Passport

Military IDs and passports, while acceptable, are not commonly used forms of identification in most areas. For this reason, you should always use an ID checking guide to validate them.

In some jurisdictions, an immigration card is an acceptable form of identification. Ask your manager if you can accept them.

IDs that are valid in one state may not be valid in another. For example, some jurisdictions do not acknowledge out-of-state drivers' licenses or state ID cards as acceptable forms of ID. Check with your manager.

In most states, the following forms of ID are ***not*** acceptable:

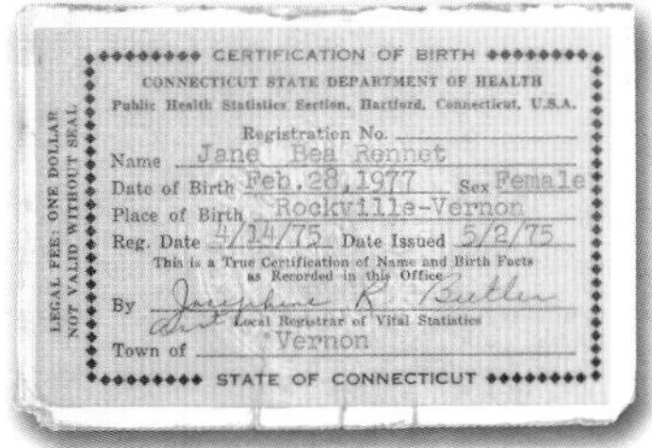

Birth Certificate

School ID

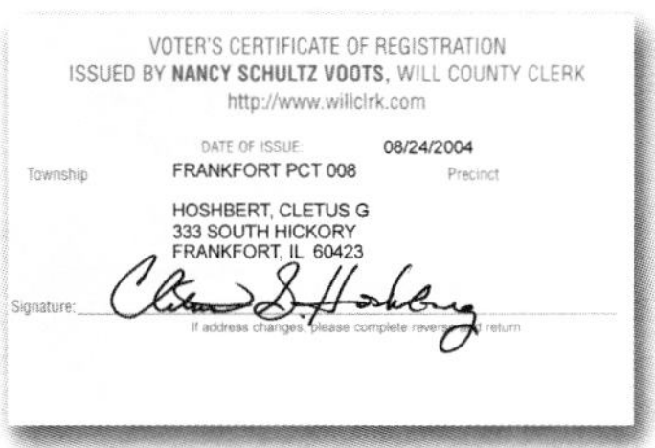

Voter's Registration Card

VERIFYING IDENTIFICATION

When checking an ID, you must verify that it

- is valid.
- has not been issued to a minor.
- is genuine.
- belongs to the guest.

Each of these topics will be discussed in detail in the following chapters.

Determining if an ID is Valid

An ID must be valid before you can accept it. A valid ID has the following features:

It contains the owner's birth date.

- The birth date can be used to calculate the age of the guest.

It is current.

- An expired license is never valid.
- Minors often use the expired license of a family member or friend who has been issued a new one.

It contains the owner's photo.

- The photo is used to verify that the person who presented the ID is the owner.

It is intact.

- Several states use IDs that are laminated, or enclosed in plastic.
- Lamination must be the proper thickness, and must not be split or contain bubbles or creases.
- In most states, a damaged ID is not valid and must be replaced.

It contains the owner's signature.

- The signature can be used to verify that the person who presented it is the owner.

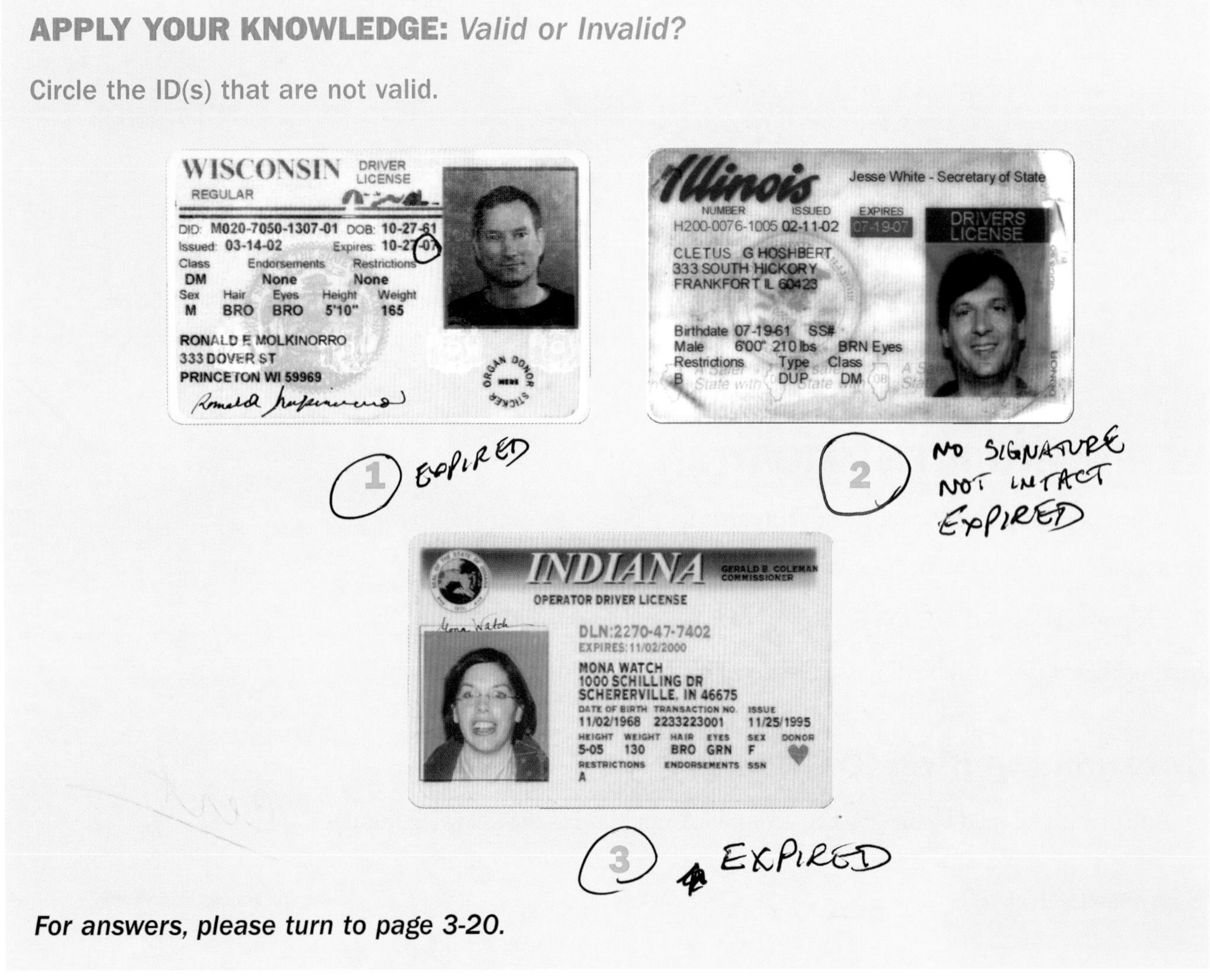

Determining if an ID Has Been Issued to a Minor

All states add special features on a minor's ID to make an underage guest easy to spot. These include:

- **Designated colors**
  - **Title bars.** Many states use specific colors in title bars, headers, and bands used to highlight text on the ID. See the ID at right.

- **Photo backdrops.** Some states use a red, yellow, or blue photo backdrop to identify minor IDs.
- **Outlines and borders around photos.** Many states use red frames, outlines, or borders around photos on minor IDs.
- **Text.** Several states display the minor's birth date, name and address, and other text in a special color.

Text

- Most states include the words, "UNDER 21," or "UNDER 21 UNTIL 00-00-0000" on the ID.

Layout features

- **Photo placement.** In some states, a minor's photo is placed on the opposite side of where it is placed for someone 21 years or older. In Minnesota, for example, a minor's photo is placed on the left side of the ID, while a person who is of age has a right-sided photo.
- **Format of the ID.** The IDs issued to minors in many states are in a vertical format rather than the horizontal format used for those 21 years of age or older.
- **Ghost photo images.** A ghost photo image is a faint copy of the photo added to the ID as a security feature. Many states place a ghost photo image on all IDs, while some states use the ghost image only on minor IDs.

HOW THIS RELATES TO ME...

List the security features used on minor IDs in your state.

MINOR IDS WITH VERTICAL FORMAT

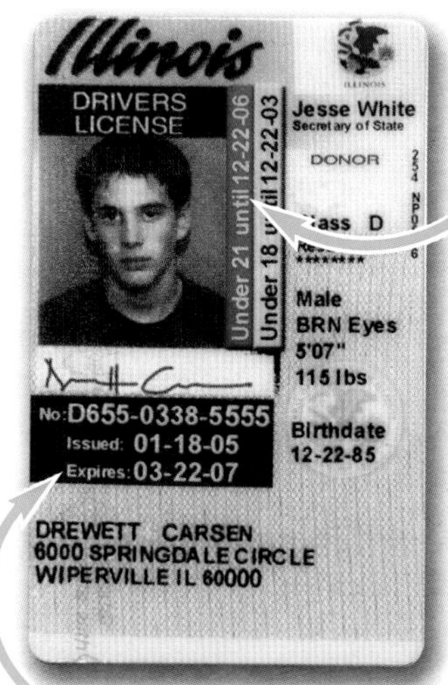

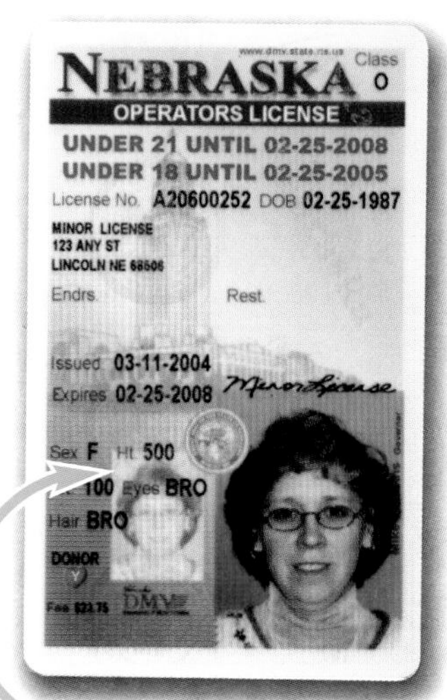

Using the Birth Date to Verify a Guest's Age

Many state IDs include the date that the minor will turn 21-years old. This eliminates the need to calculate the guest's age from his or her birth date. However, since several states do not provide this information, it is important to be able to calculate if a guest is old enough to drink.

Example: The guest was born on May 5, 1982.

Step 1 Add 20 to the guest's birth year.

1982	+ **20** =	2002
Guest's birth year		Total

Step 2 Add 1 to the total.

2002	+ **1** =	2003
Step 1 total		Calculated year

Step 3 Compare the calculated year to the current year.

2003	**to**	2004
Calculated year		Current year

IF	THEN
The calculated year occurs ***before*** the current year	The guest is ***21-years old or older.***
The calculated year occurs ***after*** the current year	The guest is ***underage.***
The calculated year ***matches*** the current year and	
■ the guest's birthday has passed	■ The guest is ***21-years old.***
■ the guest's birthday has not passed	■ The guest is ***underage.***

In the example, since the calculated year (2003) occurs before the current year (2004), the guest is 21-years old or older.

Your establishment may also post signs or calendars that state a guest must have been born on or before the current date to be served alcohol in your establishment. These can be excellent aids to help you determine if a guest is old enough to drink. They are typically available through your liquor distributor. Talk to your manager.

APPLY YOUR KNOWLEDGE: *To Serve or Not to Serve?*

It is July 19, 2004. Based on their birth dates, which of the following guests are old enough to be served?

1. Someone born on 12-31-83
2. Someone born on 01-18-84
3. Someone born on 05-11-85
4. Someone born on 07-01-82

For answers, please turn to page 3-20.

Verifying That the ID is Genuine

It is important that you become thoroughly familiar with the valid IDs in your state and neighboring states. In recent years, states have developed IDs that are difficult to alter or falsify, but counterfeiters have also become more sophisticated at creating genuine-looking IDs. The key to spotting fake IDs is to be knowledgeable and to use the most current tools at your disposal.

Check with your manager for the valid IDs issued by your state. Another important tool you can use is an ID checking guide. These guides provide full-size samples of each state's drivers' licenses. They also provide a detailed description of minor IDs, state ID cards, and valid drivers' licenses in current circulation.

Characteristics of Genuine IDs

To determine if an ID presented by a guest is genuine, look for the following characteristics:

- **Proper text and images.** The text on the ID must have the correct font and be properly spaced.

  Counterfeiters often place improper text or icons on IDs in order to avoid criminal liability. IDs should not contain the words "Official," "Valid," "Secure," "Genuine," "Authentic," "Souvenir," "Novelty," or similar terms. Also, look for improper icons such as keys or locks.

  States often include other security features on their IDs to discourage tampering. These include:

  - **Special text or images.** Several states place holograms or other images on their IDs. These images can be seen only when the ID is tilted, or they might change color or shape when the ID is held at an angle. Possible images include the state's name, seal, motto, shape, or other graphics. When checking an ID with one of these images, make sure it is appropriate, has been placed in the correct location, and is not distorted.

    Several states include objects that can only be seen using ultraviolet light. If the ID contains these features, you must make sure they are present.

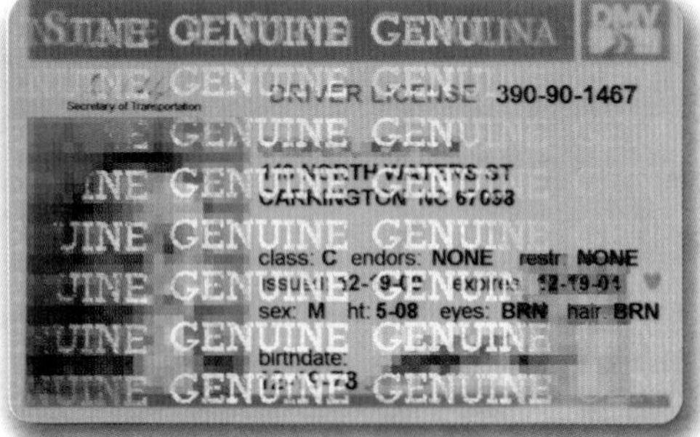

Note the word *Genuine* on this fake ID.

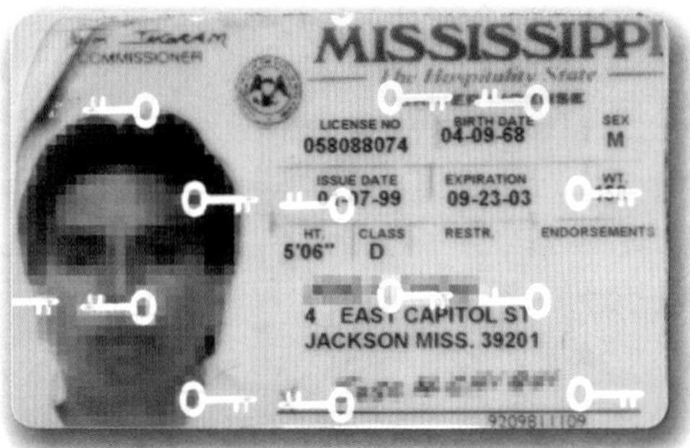

Note the image of the key on this fake ID.

  - **License numbers.** All states include a license number on the ID. This may consist of the person's social security number, or a series of letters and/or digits that may be coded to the person's name, birth date, etc. When checking IDs, make sure that this number contains the appropriate letter(s) and/or number of digits. If the number is coded to the person's personal information, make sure it is coded correctly.

- **Clear photos.** A blurry photo may indicate that the ID has been altered. Many states include a ghost photo image on the ID as an additional security feature. When checking IDs from these states, make sure the ghost image is present and matches the photo.
- **Appropriate information on the back.** All state-issued ID cards contain information on the back, such as an organ-donor signature area or driving restrictions. A majority of states also include bar codes, magnetic stripes, or both on the back of their IDs. These contain specific data about the person, and can be accessed by using an ID reader (see page 3-16). For states that include bar codes and/or magnetic stripes, make sure these features are present on the ID.

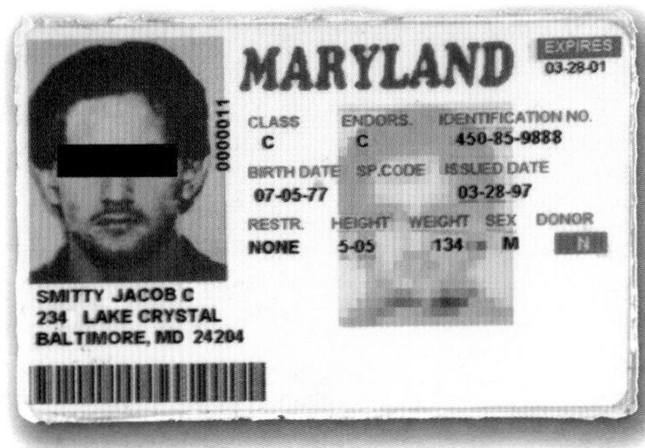

This fake ID has a blurry photo, indicating that it has been altered.

You should be aware that the backs of fake IDs are sometimes blank or contain a statement that identifies it as a fake, such as "For Entertainment Purposes Only." For this reason, always check the back of an ID to ensure it is genuine.

APPLY YOUR KNOWLEDGE: *Check It Out!*

Using this page from the *I.D. Checking Guide,* identify the features on the ID that should be verified to ensure the ID is genuine.

For answers, please turn to page 3-20.

NEBRASKA

Description: Current license is digitized with ghost image; 2D bar code on back. Prior license: Photographic, encased in plastic. Current CDL shows "COMMERCIAL DRIVERS LICENSE" in orange headbar. Prior license has "COMMERCIAL/DRIVERS LICENSE" at top right of state heading.

Minor's license: Current in vertical format with "UNDER 21 UNTIL MM-DD-YYYY" and, if applicable, "UNDER 18 UNTIL MM-DD-YYYY" in red under headbar. Prior licenses issued beginning September 1999 have a red photo backdrop and "UNDER 21" down each side and on the back. Blue "MINOR" stickers, begun in September 1997, are no longer issued.

Validation: Current license: Front laminate shows an optically variable pattern of the state name and seal that changes color when the license is tilted and that fluoresces under UV light. Date of birth overlaps ghost image; state seal overlaps photo and ghost image. Prior license: State seal and 3-digit serial number below state seal overlap photo. Laminate contains a box with "BUCKLE UP (with or without) NEBRASKA" and "DON'T DRINK AND DRIVE" over data portion.

License number: One letter followed by up to 8 numbers, not spaced, not coded.

License term: Up to 5 years, expiring on birthday in the 5th year after issuance, making the license good for up to 5 years 11 months. If under 21, license expires on 21st birthday.

I.D. Checking Guide page courtesy of The Drivers License Company.

HOW THIS RELATES TO ME...

List the security features used on IDs issued by your state.

____

____

____

____

Verifying That the ID Belongs to the Guest

A common practice used by minors is to present the valid ID of a family member or friend. They might also use an expired license from an individual who has been issued a new one.

To verify that the ID belongs to a guest:

- **Compare the guest to the photo on the ID.** When making the comparison, you should account for changes that may have occurred since the photo was taken, such as differences in hair length/color, facial hair, etc. Look at the chin, nose, eyes, eyebrows, hairline, and shape of the guest's face. They should match the features in the photo.

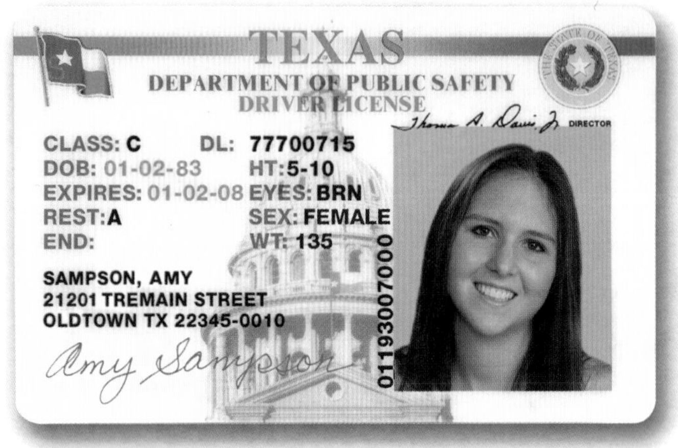

- **Compare the guest to the physical characteristics listed on the ID.**
  Make sure the following features match:

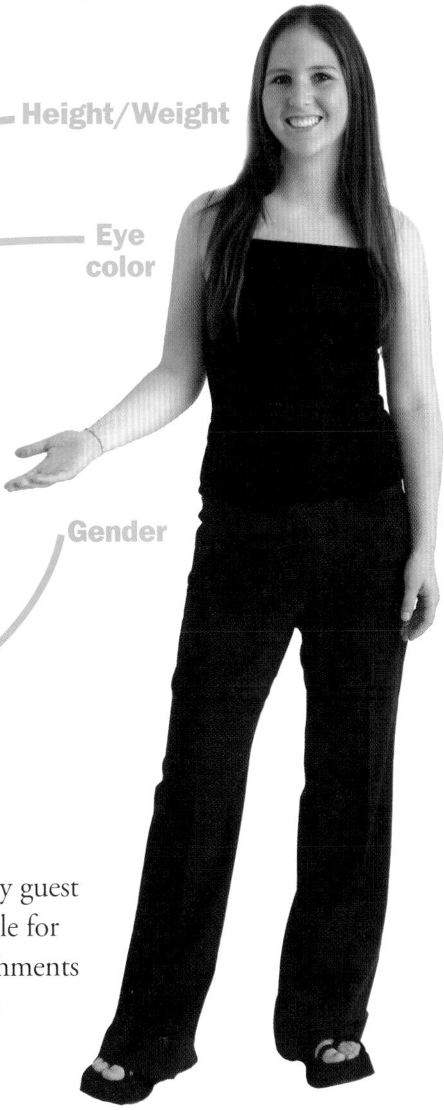

Height/Weight

Eye color

Gender

WHEN TO CHECK IDs

Since it is illegal to serve alcohol to a minor, it is vital that you card any guest that appears to be under 21 years of age. Remember: you can be held liable for your failure to do so. To take the guesswork out of carding, many establishments require staff to card guests who are clearly older than 21 years of age—for example 25- or 30-years old. Always follow your house policies regarding when to card.

HOW THIS RELATES TO ME...

When should IDs be checked in your establishment?

THE PROPER PROCEDURE FOR CHECKING IDs

IDs must be checked thoroughly and properly according to the procedure below. While this may seem like an inconvenience, especially during a rush, you must never skip steps. Any time guests leave the establishment and then return, you should recheck their IDs. If you are in doubt or not comfortable with the situation, contact your manager. ***You have the legal right to refuse service if you suspect the guest is a minor.***

Greet the guest politely.

The greeting can help you assess whether the guest

- is nervous (avoiding eye contact), indicating that he or she may be using a fake ID.

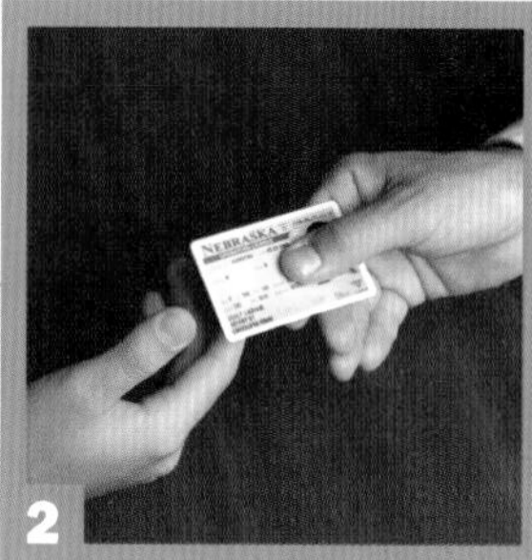

Politely ask the guest for ID.

Ask the guest to remove the ID from his or her wallet. Hold the ID to detect signs of tampering, including:

- Bubbles and creases
- Improper thickness
- Ink signatures

Signs of tampering may be easier to spot if you light the ID from behind while examining it.

Greet the guest using the name on the ID to

- discourage the guest from lending the ID to another guest.
- remind you later that you've checked this ID.

Verify the ID.

Make sure it

- is valid.
- has not been issued to a minor.
- is genuine.
- belongs to the guest.

Is the ID OK

YES

UNSURE

4

Seek further verification.

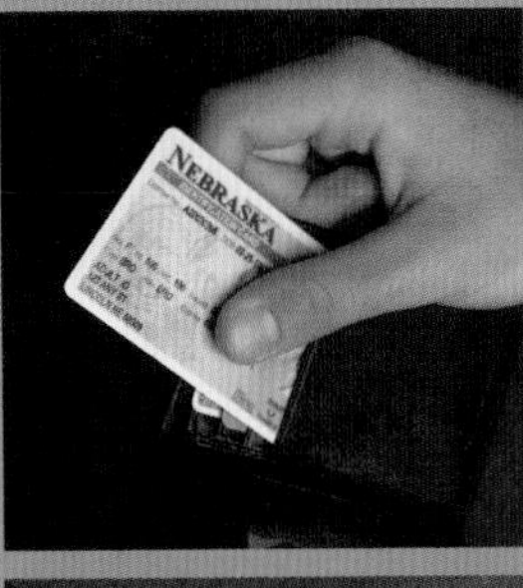

- Ask the guest for a second valid ID.

AND/OR

- Compare the guest's signature to the ID signature.

AND/OR

- Ask the guest questions only the ID owner could answer, including:
  - What is your address?
  - How tall are you?
  - What is your middle name?
  - In what month were you born?

Is the ID OK

NO

Refuse service.

Whenever you refuse service to a minor, notify your manager.

Be firm, but always express regret. Do not

- sound authoritative or judgmental.
- embarrass the minor.

You might say something like:

- "I'm sorry, but it's illegal to serve a minor."
- "I'm sorry, but I can't serve you without a valid ID."
- "I'm sorry, but our company policy will not allow me to serve you."

YES

Serve the guest.

APPLY YOUR KNOWLEDGE: *Spot the Fake*

Circle the ID(s) that are fake.

1

2

3

For answers, please turn to page 3-20.

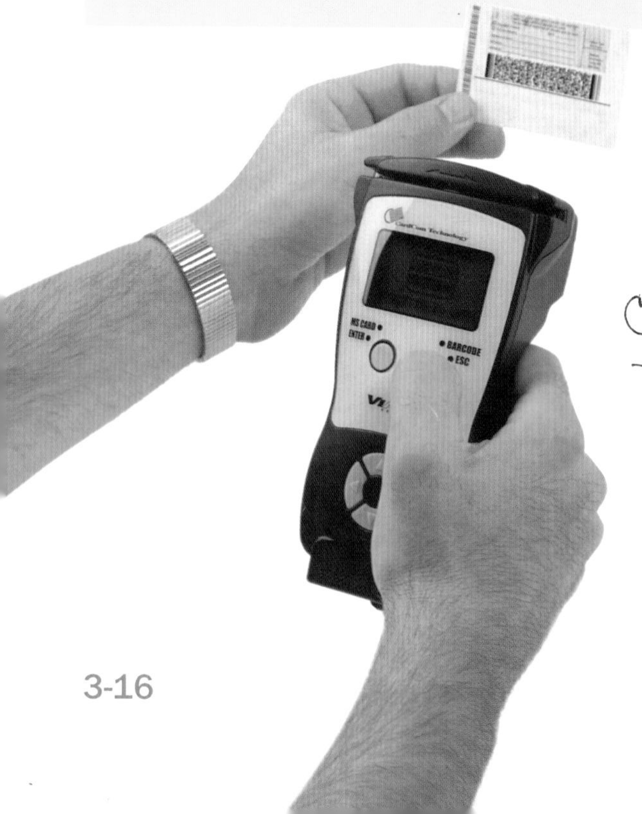

USING ID READERS

Some establishments use ID readers to check IDs with bar codes or magnetic stripes. While these tools can help verify the age of a guest, they should be used along with the other checking procedures discussed in this chapter. It is especially important to compare the ID reader's display with the actual information listed on the ID, since bar codes can be imported from valid ID cards. If the ID contains magnetic stripes, the stripes should be checked for signs of tampering intended to invalidate the reading.

DEALING WITH A FAKE ID

If you spot a fake ID, there are several steps you can take depending upon your company policy and the law in your jurisdiction. This may include refusing service, refusing entry to your establishment, and/or confiscating the ID. Always follow your company policy.

APPLY YOUR KNOWLEDGE: *Rate the Response*

This activity requires the Video/DVD 5: *Evaluating Real-World Scenarios.* After watching each scenario from Section 2 of this video/DVD, rate how well the employee handled the situation by placing the appropriate number in the space provided.

Rating Scale
1 = Employee handled the situation effectively.
2 = Employee handled the situation somewhat effectively.
3 = Employee handled the situation ineffectively.

Video Segment	Description	Rating
1	Parents attempting to serve an underage child in a fine-dining restaurant	
2	Group of friends attempting to enter a nightclub	
3	Flirtatious guest attempting to be served at the bar	
4	Guests attempting to enter a nightclub	
5	Guest attempting to be served at a sports bar	

For answers, please turn to page 3-21.

SUMMARY

As a seller or server of alcohol, you are responsible for ensuring that your guests are of legal age to drink. If you serve an underage guest, you can be held criminally liable. Remember: you have the legal right to refuse service if you suspect the guest is underage. Always follow your company policies.

The type of identification that can be used to confirm a guest's age depends upon what is legally acceptable in your state or municipality. In most states, this includes a driver's license, state ID card, passport, and military ID. When checking an ID, you must make sure it is valid, has not been issued to a minor, is genuine, and belongs to the guest who presented it. A valid ID is intact and current and contains the owner's photograph, signature, and birth date.

States place certain features on minor IDs to make an underage guest easy to spot. This includes the use of designated colors, text, and specific layout features. Many states also show on the ID the date that the minor will be 21-years old. This eliminates the need to calculate the guest's age from his or her birth date. However, since a number of states still do not provide this information, you must be able to make this calculation.

To determine if an ID is genuine, make sure that it contains the proper text and images, a clear photo, and the appropriate information on the back side. Check with your manager for information on the valid IDs issued by your state, and use an ID checking guide. To verify that an ID belongs to a guest, compare the guest to the photo and the physical characteristics listed on the ID.

When checking an ID, start by politely greeting the guest. This can help you assess whether the individual is nervous—a sign he or she may be underage. Next, politely ask the guest to remove the ID from his or her wallet. Once you have looked at the name, greet the guest using it. This can discourage the individual from lending the ID to another guest, and it can help remind you later that you have already checked the ID. It is also important to hold the ID, since this can help you spot signs of tampering. Verify the ID by making sure it is valid, has not been issued to a minor, is genuine, and belongs to the guest. Seek further clarification if you are unsure that the ID is valid. You can ask the guest for a second ID, compare the individual's signature to the signature on the ID, or ask a question only the guest could answer. If you are still unsure that the ID is valid, refuse service and inform your manager. If you spot a fake ID, always follow your company policy.

If your establishment uses an ID reader to check IDs with bar codes or magnetic stripes, make sure you always compare the display with the actual information listed on the ID. Do not rely solely on the ID reader. ID readers should be used in addition to the other checking procedures identified in this chapter.

MULTIPLE-CHOICE STUDY QUESTIONS

?

1. **Which of the following forms of identification is acceptable for verifying a guest's age?**
   - A. School ID
   - B. Passport
   - C. Birth certificate
   - D. Voter registration card

2. **To be valid, an ID must have all of the following features *except* a**
   - A. birth date.
   - B. photo.
   - C. hologram.
   - D. signature.

3. **All of the following features are used by states to indicate that an ID belongs to a minor *except***
   - A. placing the words "Secure," "Genuine," or "Valid" on the ID.
   - B. orienting the ID in a vertical format.
   - C. highlighting the birth date in a different color.
   - D. placing the photo on the side opposite of where it is placed for those over 21 years of age.

4. **All of the following are grounds for rejecting an ID *except***
   - A. split lamination.
   - B. improperly spaced text.
   - C. a ghost photo image on the ID.
   - D. a blank back side.

5. **What should you do to verify that an ID belongs to the guest?**
   - A. Check for splits in the lamination.
   - B. Verify the state seal is in the proper location.
   - C. Compare the guest to the physical characteristics listed on the ID.
   - D. Check the license number to see if the coding matches the personal information.

6. **After asking for a guest's ID, why should you greet the individual using the name on the ID?**
   - A. It helps you determine if the ID is valid.
   - B. It prevents you from having to card the guest again later.
   - C. It discourages the guest from lending the ID to another guest.
   - D. It reduces your liability in the event that you miss something.

For answers, please turn to page 3-21.

ANSWERS

Page	Activity
3-2	Test Your Knowledge 1. False 2. False 3. True 4. True 5. True
3-3	Spot the Minor All of them are minors.
3-6	Valid or Invalid? ID #2 is not valid because it is missing a signature and is not intact. ID #3 is not valid because it has expired.
3-9	To Serve or Not to Serve? Only #4 is over 21 years of age.
3-11	Check It Out! 1. The ID must contain a ghost image. 2. The license must contain a two-dimensional bar code on the back. 3. The date of birth must overlap the ghost image. 4. The state name and seal must appear in a repeating pattern that changes color when the license is tilted and fluoresces under UV light. 5. The state seal must overlap the photo and ghost image. 6. The license number must contain one letter followed by eight numbers that are not spaced or coded.
3-16	Spot the Fake Both ID #1 and ID #3 are fakes. ID #1 has the word "authentic" on it, while the word "secure" and pictures of locks can be see on ID #3. ID #3 also has an incorrectly colored photo background.

Continued on next page...

ANSWERS continued

Page	Activity

3-17 Rate the Response

1. Rating: 1—Effective

   Here is how the server handled the situation effectively:

   - He was not authoritative when refusing service.
   - He quoted the law and the consequences to both himself and the establishment when denying service.
   - He was firm in the decision to refuse service.

2. Rating: 1—Effective

   Here is how the valet handled the situation effectively:

   - He communicated important information to the doorman who was checking IDs.

   Here is how the doorman handled the situation effectively:

   - He thoroughly examined the ID to ensure it was genuine.
   - Since he was unsure if the ID belonged to the guest, he asked appropriate questions to verify it, including asking to compare the guest's signature with the signature on the ID.
   - He was polite when refusing entry.

3. Rating: 3—Ineffective

   The bartender made the following mistakes:

   - The bartender failed to use an ID checking guide to examine the out-of-state ID.
   - The bartender failed to notice that the photo did not match the guest. This should have prompted a more thorough examination of the ID.
   - The bartender failed to notice that the back of the ID was blank, indicating it was a fake.

4. Rating: 3—Ineffective

   The doorman made the following mistake:

   - The doorman failed to compare the readouts on the ID reader with the information on the IDs.

5. Rating: 3—Ineffective

   The bartender made the following mistakes:

   - The bartender failed to notice that the guest appeared nervous.
   - The bartender failed to ask the guest to remove his ID from his wallet.

3-19 Multiple-Choice Study Questions

1. B
2. C
3. A
4. C
5. C
6. C

Handling Difficult Situations

After completing this chapter, you should be able to:

- Identify the procedure for stopping alcohol service to a guest.
- Identify the procedure for handling intoxicated guests who attempt to leave the premises.
- Identify the procedure for handling a guest who has arrived at the establishment intoxicated.
- Identify the procedure for handling designated drivers.
- Identify the procedure for handling potentially violent situations.
- Identify the procedure for handling illegal activities.
- Identify the procedure servers should follow if asked to perform an illegal activity.
- Identify incidents that require documentation.

TEST YOUR KNOWLEDGE

1. **True or False:** When stopping alcohol service to a guest, the backup person should stand as close to the guest as possible. *(See page 4-3.)*
2. **True or False:** Using statements such as *"You've had enough,"* when stopping service will deflect blame from you and defuse the situation. *(See page 4-4.)*
3. **True or False:** You should call the police if an intoxicated guest insists on driving away from the establishment. *(See page 4-9.)*
4. **True or False:** Guests can be served to the point of intoxication if they are traveling with a designated driver. *(See page 4-11.)*
5. **True or False:** You should physically restrain a violent guest so he or she does not cause injury. *(See page 4-12.)*

For answers, please turn to page 4-20.

INTRODUCTION

From time to time you may be confronted with situations that are difficult to handle. It is important for you to remember that your personal safety comes first. If you feel threatened or are concerned that you may be in danger, remove yourself from the situation and notify a manager or the owner.

HANDLING INTOXICATED GUESTS

Despite your best efforts, guests may still become intoxicated. How you handle these situations is very important. It starts with the decision to stop service.

Stopping Service to Intoxicated Guests

If a guest is showing physical or behavioral signs of intoxication, or you are concerned about the number of drinks he or she has consumed, you must stop serving alcohol. Some establishments allow employees to stop service but require them to notify management, while others require management to stop service.

When stopping service to a guest:

Always alert a backup before stopping service.

Ask an accompanying friend or relative to help you stop service to a guest.

1. **Alert a backup:** The backup person should be prepared to provide assistance, and must be close enough to observe the situation, but not so close to appear threatening to the guest.
2. **Enlist the help of other guests if possible:** There are times when you may be able to convince an accompanying friend or relative to help you stop service. For example, if the intoxicated guest steps away, tell the friend or relative that you must stop service, and ask for help. The companion may be able to intervene and convince the guest not to order another drink. Companions may also be able to smooth over the situation if you must stop service.
3. **Wait until the guest orders the next round before stopping service:** Sometimes a guest may decide that his or her current drink is the last, and you will be able to avoid a delicate situation. Notifying a guest that you are stopping service while serving him or her a final drink can upset the guest and allow time to build resentment over your decision.

4. **Inform the guest you are stopping service:** Keep the conversation as private and non-confrontational as possible. To prevent a confrontation:

Express concern and empathy when stopping service to a guest.

- **Avoid being judgmental.** Don't use *"You"* statements. Saying *"You've had enough,"* or *"You're drunk,"* sounds judgmental and may offend the guest. Instead, use statements such as *"I'm not able to serve you any more alcohol this evening,"* or *"Our company policy doesn't allow me to serve you any more alcohol."* Tell the guest that the establishment is responsible if something should occur. Explain that it is against the law to serve any more alcohol. These types of statements help deflect blame from the guest and you, and help defuse the situation. Practice these interventions until they become natural for you.
- **Express concern.** Be genuine. Tell the guest that you are concerned about his or her safety. Saying something like *"I just want to make sure you get home OK,"* is effective and helps guests see that you care about them.
- **Express empathy.** Show the guest you understand how he or she is feeling. This might include saying something like, *"I know this is frustrating or annoying, but I am concerned about your safety."* Make sure that you maintain eye contact while you talk to the guest, and nod and shake your head when appropriate. This will show that you are listening.
- **Be firm.** Guests will often try to persuade you to change your mind, or ask for *"just one more"* drink. Once you have made the decision to stop service, stick to it. Remember: it is against the law to serve an intoxicated guest. Be patient and remain calm. Simply and clearly repeat your decision to stop alcohol service as often as necessary.

5. **Offer nonalcoholic alternatives:** Offer the guest coffee, soft drinks, or other nonalcoholic alternatives. This will allow time for the guest's body to process the alcohol he or she has consumed. If the guest came into the establishment with friends, it will also allow him or her to still feel like a part of the group.

You may stop service to a guest, only to find that the individual is still getting drinks from companions. Immediately stop service to all of the guests and remove the alcohol from the table.

If drinks are being passed to underage guests, the situation must be handled in the same way—alcohol service must be stopped. Keep in mind, however, that in some states it is legal for parents or legal guardians to serve a minor. Ask your manager if this is legal in your state.

When stopping service to a guest, offer nonalcoholic alternatives.

Stopping Service to Regulars

There are times when it may be necessary to stop service to a "regular." This can sometimes be intimidating, especially when the guest has been coming to the establishment for a long time or when a friendship has developed between the two of you. Never let this get in the way of doing the right thing! When guests have had enough, they have had enough, regardless of their patronage. Let your relationship work to your advantage. Express the genuine concern you have for their safety, but be firm.

HOW THIS RELATES TO ME...

What is your company policy for stopping service to a guest?

APPLY YOUR KNOWLEDGE: *Am I Saying That Right?*

Write *Yes* next to the statement if you think it is appropriate when stopping service to a guest or *No* if it is not.

1. Yes "I'm sorry, but I don't feel comfortable serving you another drink. How about a soda or a cup of coffee instead?"
2. NO "This is the last drink I can serve you this evening."
3. NO "We feel you've had enough, and it's against our policy to serve you any more alcohol."
4. Yes "I'm sorry, but I could get fired if I serve you another drink."
5. NO "I think you've had enough, sir."
6. NO "I'm not sure you can make it home, so I really can't serve you another drink."
7. NO "You're not getting another drink because I think you're intoxicated."
8. NO "I guess I can serve you another beer, but this will have to be the last one."
9. Yes "Sir, I am going to have to stop serving your friend. Can you make that drink your last drink and see that he gets home safely?"
10. Yes "I'm sorry, but it is against the law for me to serve you any more alcohol."

For answers, please turn to page 4-20.

HOW THIS RELATES TO ME...

List statements you have used that have been successful when stopping service to a guest.

SOMETHING TO THINK ABOUT...

Alex, a regular at Walker's Steakhouse, sat at the restaurant's bar. He had been there for hours having several drinks and a few light appetizers. In the last hour, Alex switched from drinking Manhattans to beer and double shots of whiskey. As he became increasingly loud, using foul language and slurring his speech, Marlon, the bartender, became concerned. Marlon knew that Alex was a valued customer and a friend of the owner, so he decided to inform his general manager about the situation.

Chris, the general manager, consulted with the restaurant's owner. Neither of them wanted to stop service because Alex brought a lot of business to the establishment. Instead, they decided to follow Alex home, since he lived close by. Chris agreed to use his car to follow Alex home.

Chris drove closely behind Alex, keeping Alex's car in sight. Just as they both safely made it through an intersection, however, Alex swerved and swiped the side of a parked car. He continued on his way without even noticing what he had done.

What do you think of the decision to follow Alex home? What should have been done differently?

SOMETHING TO THINK ABOUT...

Guests drinking at multiple establishments, or "bar hopping," is an important issue that servers must keep in mind when serving alcohol. In a recent case, a woman was killed and her two-year old daughter was severely injured when their car was hit by a drunk driver who had moved from bar to bar over a period of eight hours. By the time he began driving home, the man had consumed over 15 drinks at three establishments.

In the subsequent civil lawsuit brought by the victims' family, all three establishments were named liable, including one where the man had consumed only one drink. During the trial, a bartender from the third establishment claimed to notice that the man had arrived intoxicated and thus had been refused service; however, the bartender did not secure alternate transportation and the man returned to his car. The victims' family was awarded over one million dollars in damages.

Handling Intoxicated Guests Attempting to Leave the Premises*

Once you have stopped service to a guest, the next step is to ensure that the person gets home safely. Sometimes the intoxicated guest will have driven to your establishment with a companion. If these people have remained sober, you may be able to enlist their help in driving the guest home. However, the situation can become much more challenging when the guest has driven to your establishment alone.

There are several important steps to follow to prevent an intoxicated guest from driving. Whatever you do, never use physical force to try to stop the guest.

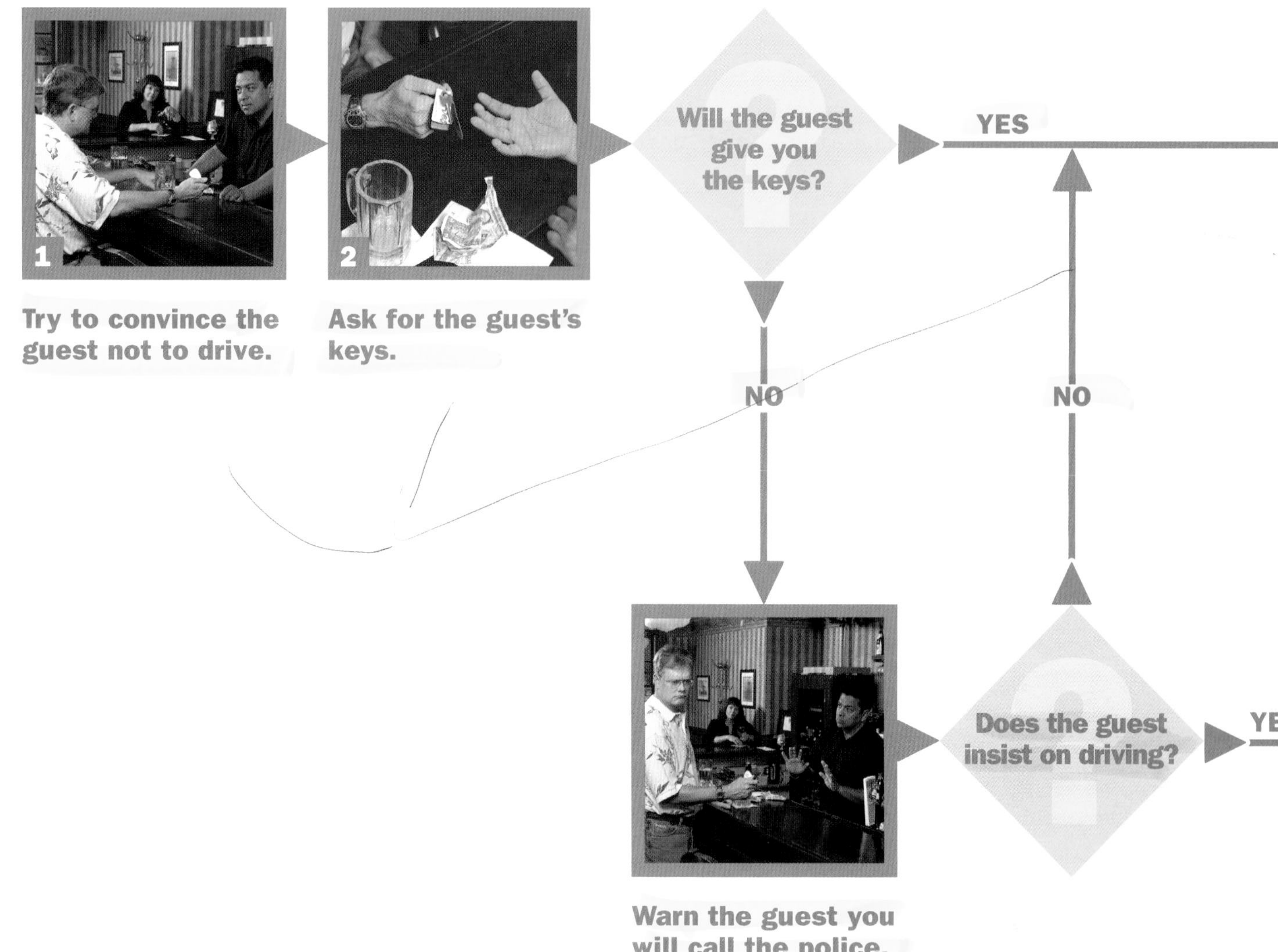

*Always follow company policy when handling these situations.

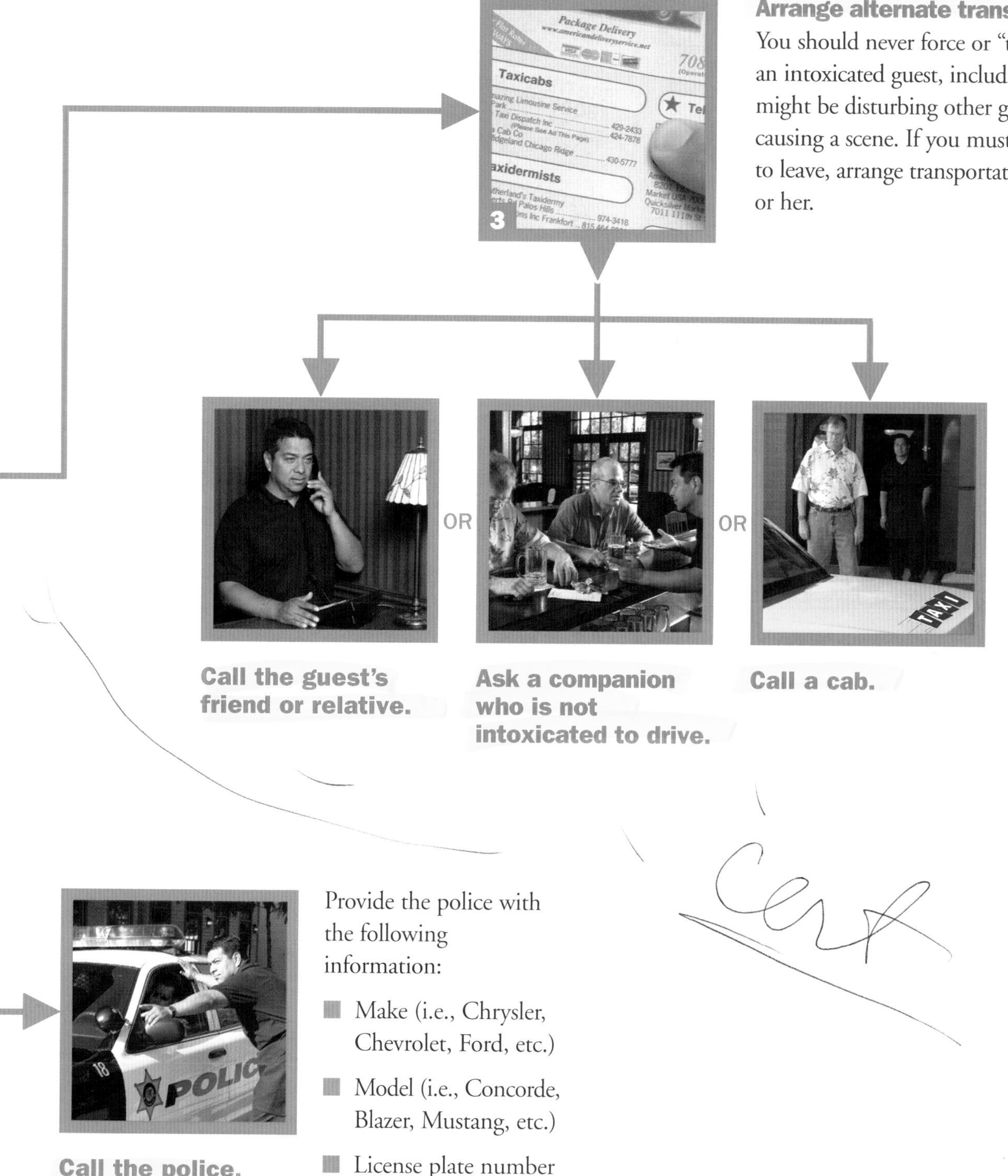

Arrange alternate transportation. You should never force or "throw out" an intoxicated guest, including one who might be disturbing other guests or causing a scene. If you must ask a guest to leave, arrange transportation for him or her.

Call the guest's friend or relative.

Ask a companion who is not intoxicated to drive.

Call a cab.

Call the police.

Provide the police with the following information:

- Make (i.e., Chrysler, Chevrolet, Ford, etc.)
- Model (i.e., Concorde, Blazer, Mustang, etc.)
- License plate number
- Direction the guest was heading

HOW THIS RELATES TO ME...

What does your establishment do to ensure that an intoxicated guest gets home safely?

Dealing with Guests Who Arrive Intoxicated

If guests are intoxicated when they arrive at your establishment, try to refuse entry. If they come inside, make sure they are not served any alcohol by communicating this information to all appropriate coworkers. Remember: while you have not served the intoxicated guest, you should take steps to keep that person from leaving in that condition. Ask the guest for his or her keys. If refused, tell the guest that you will call the police if he or she attempts to drive away. If the guest still insists on driving—call the police! If the guest has agreed not to drive, ask if you can call a friend or relative to provide a ride. If no one is available, call a cab.

If guests are intoxicated when they arrive at the establishment, try to refuse entry.

HOW THIS RELATES TO ME...

How does your establishment handle guests who arrive intoxicated?

Designated Drivers

Some establishments use a designated driver program to aid in the responsible service of alcohol. In this program, one person in a group of drinkers consents to be the designated driver and agrees not to consume alcohol during the visit. In exchange, he or she is usually offered complimentary food, nonalcoholic beverages, or other incentives, such as coupons for future visits.

Many guests mistakenly believe that they will be allowed to drink to the point of intoxication if they come to the establishment with a designated driver. Nothing is farther from the truth. As a seller or server of alcohol, you are still liable for overserving a guest even if a designated driver is present. Let guests know that despite the presence of a designated driver, you cannot overserve them. You don't know where the designated driver will be taking them next—whether that is home, to another establishment, or to their cars.

Throughout the group's visit, you should encourage the designated driver to abstain from drinking alcohol. If the individual chooses to start drinking, monitor his or her consumption like you would any other guest. For designated drivers who fulfill their commitment not to drink, follow your company policy regarding the distribution of incentives.

HANDLING POTENTIALLY VIOLENT SITUATIONS

Unfortunately, there are times when you may be exposed to potentially violent situations. This may include everything from guests who display behavior that is unruly, inappropriate, threatening, or abusive, to assaults, fights, and staff violence. In most states, the law requires you to make a reasonable effort to anticipate problems and prevent injury.

Involving a manager early on will give you the opportunity to make the best decision when handling a situation.

To prevent injury when handling potentially violent situations:

- **Notify your manager.** If you pay close attention to your guests, you will be aware of potential problems that may be developing. Involving your manager early on will give you the opportunity to determine the best way to handle the situation.

- **Call the police.** Sometimes you are caught by surprise, or are too busy to notice a problem before it has developed into a potentially violent situation. This is the time to call the police! Do not assume that the situation will resolve itself. It usually won't. You must call the police whenever your safety or the safety of others is at risk.

Call the police whenever safety is at risk.

- **Separate guests from the situation.** This will help prevent them from being injured.
- **Never touch or try to physically restrain a violent guest.**

Try to separate guests from violent situations.

HOW THIS RELATES TO ME...

How does your establishment require you to handle potentially violent situations?

HANDLING ILLEGAL ACTIVITIES

There are times when you may witness illegal activities in your establishment, such as gambling, prostitution, or the possession or sale of drugs on the premises. It is against the law to allow these activities to continue on the premises. When faced with these situations, you should do the following:

- **Consider your safety and the safety of your guests before taking action.**
- **Notify your manager.** He or she will determine the type of intervention that is required.
- **Call the police.**

Some situations require you to exercise extreme caution, such as handling a guest who is carrying a weapon (in states where it is illegal to do so). In addition to the suggestions listed above, never confront a guest with a weapon.

HOW THIS RELATES TO ME...

How does your establishment handle illegal activities?

SOMETHING TO THINK ABOUT...

On a busy Friday night at Barry's BBQ, Quinn, one of the restaurant's bartenders, took a quick break. He stepped outside for some air. In the parking lot behind the establishment, Quinn noticed a young couple, a blonde woman and a dark-haired man, hunched over the hood of a car. They appeared to be taking turns at something. Quinn couldn't quite see what they were doing, but he thought it might be drugs. He hurried inside to get back to the bar, but since he wasn't sure about what he saw in the parking lot, Quinn decided not to say anything to his manager.

About an hour later, Quinn noticed the woman from the parking lot again, this time seated at the end of bar. She was talking loudly and acting aggressively toward another patron, Tim—a frequent diner at the restaurant. Her companion stood nearby and was also visibly angry. Quinn knew that Tim was a quiet guy who had never been involved in a confrontation at the restaurant. He watched in horror as Tim, who tried to back away from the couple, was tackled to the floor by the man, while the woman began to kick Tim's midsection and head.

Though the fight was stopped and the couple was arrested, Tim suffered severe injuries. Toxicology tests revealed that there were traces of cocaine in the bloodstreams of the couple at the time of the assault.

What should Quinn have done differently?

Management Support

When handling situations in which you have a legal responsibility, such as stopping service to an intoxicated guest, you should always involve your manager. There may be times, however, when the manager may not agree with your decision. When this happens, remember that you are liable for your actions while serving alcohol. If you are not comfortable with what your manager has asked you to do, express your concern. If he or she insists, ask the manager to do it instead. If you feel that you are being asked to do something that is against the law, such as continuing to serve visibly intoxicated guests, talk to the owner or your human resources department.

APPLY YOUR KNOWLEDGE: *Rate the Response*

This activity requires Video/DVD 5:, *Evaluating Real-World Scenarios.* After watching each scenario from Section 3 of this video, use the rating scale below to rate how well the employee handled each situation by placing the appropriate number in the space provided.

Rating Scale
1 = Employee handled the situation effectively.
2 = Employee handled the situation somewhat effectively.
3 = Employee handled the situation ineffectively.

Video Segment	Description	Rating
1	Male guest entering an establishment	
2	Two female guests dining in a fine-dining restaurant	
3	Valet interacting with a guest leaving the establishment	
4	Two male guests watching a football game at a bar	
5	Female guest talking with a bartender at the bar	
6	Regular interacting with a bartender at the bar	
7	Guest talking to a female server at the end of the bar	
8	Bartender interacting with a guest in the restroom	
9	Group of friends with a designated driver	
10	Server interacting with a softball team	

For answers, please turn to page 4-20.

APPLY YOUR KNOWLEDGE: *Put It into Practice*

Now it is time to put together everything you have learned by practicing how to handle a difficult situation.

1. Choose a partner. Together, create a realistic scenario in which an employee must handle a difficult situation with a guest.
2. Act out the scenario in front of the group, with one of you playing the employee and the other playing the guest. Draw on your experience, or on things you may have witnessed in an alcohol-service situation.
3. As an audience member, provide constructive feedback for the other scenarios presented. As a group, discuss how well the employee handled the situation.

DOCUMENTING INCIDENTS

When an incident occurs on the premises, your establishment may require you to complete an incident report, which is used to document what happened and what actions were taken. These reports help your organization determine if policies are effective or whether they need to be revised. You should provide accurate information, and fill out the report immediately so important facts are not forgotten. Closely follow your company policy on what to include and how to document the incident.

If your establishment documents incidents, reports should be completed when

- alcohol service has been stopped to a guest.
- alternate transportation has been arranged for a guest.
- a guest's ID has been confiscated.

- an illegal activity or violent situation has occurred.
- a guest has become ill.

SUMMARY

When a guest shows signs of intoxication, stop serving alcohol. Begin by alerting a backup. Whenever possible, enlist the help of a guest's companions. Wait until the guest orders another round before refusing service. Keep the conversation as private and non-confrontational as possible. Avoid being judgmental, but be firm. Be empathetic and express concern. Finally, offer the guest nonalcoholic alternatives.

Once you have stopped alcohol service, you must make sure the guest gets home safely. Sometimes you can ask an accompanying friend or relative to drive the individual home. If the guest is alone, try to convince him or her not to drive, and ask for car keys. If the guest gives them to you, find alternate transportation—this can include calling a cab. Warn the guest that if he or she insists on driving, you will call the police. Do it if the guest persists. Whatever you do, never use physical force to try to stop a guest from driving.

Unfortunately, you may have to deal with potentially violent situations. To prevent injury, you should anticipate problems and notify your manager before the situation becomes violent. If you are caught by surprise and violence is likely to occur, call the police. Try to separate other guests from the situation. Never touch or attempt to physically restrain a guest.

If an incident does occur on the premises, you may be required to complete a report documenting what happened and the actions taken. Ask your manager about your company's policy regarding incident reporting and follow it closely.

MULTIPLE-CHOICE STUDY QUESTIONS

?

1. **Which of the following statements about stopping service to a guest is *not* true?**
   A. You should wait until the guest orders another round before refusing service.
   B. You should give the guest another drink if it will prevent a confrontation.
   C. You should tell the guest that it's against the law for you to serve any more alcohol.
   D. You should ask an accompanying friend or relative to help you stop service.

2. **Which of the following statements should be avoided when stopping service to a guest?**
   A. *"You've had enough."*
   B. *"I just want to make sure you get home OK."*
   C. *"Our company policy does not allow me to serve you any more alcohol."*
   D. *"It's against the law for me to serve you any more alcohol."*

3. **To prevent an intoxicated guest from driving, you should**
   A. have the guest's car towed.
   B. warn the guest that you will call the police.
   C. physically stop the guest from getting into the car.
   D. physically stop the guest from leaving the establishment.

4. **If a guest is intoxicated upon arriving at the establishment, you should**
   A. refuse entry to the establishment.
   B. ask for the guest's car keys.
   C. arrange alternate transportation.
   D. All of the above

5. **Which of the following statements about designated drivers is true?**
   A. Overserving a guest, even if accompanied by a designated driver, is illegal.
   B. Guests can be allowed to drink to the point of intoxication if accompanied by a designated driver.
   C. A server is not liable for overserving a guest who was accompanied by a designated driver.
   D. Establishments are not liable for overserving guests who are accompanied by a designated driver.

Continued on next page...

MULTIPLE-CHOICE STUDY QUESTIONS *continued*

?

6. **If a fight occurs, you should**
   A. leave the room.
   B. attempt to physically restrain the guests.
   C. separate other guests from the situation.
   D. wait and see if the situation resolves itself.

7. **Which of the following situations *does not* require an incident report?**
   A. You witness a drug transaction at the bar.
   B. You card a guest you think is underage.
   C. You call an ambulance for a guest who has become dizzy.
   D. You stop serving alcohol to a guest you think is intoxicated.

8. **You have decided to stop alcohol service to a group of guests, but your manager has told you to continue serving them. You should do all of the following *except***
   A. serve the guests.
   B. ask the manager to serve the guests.
   C. express your concern to the manager.
   D. talk to the owner or your human resources department.

9. **When handling a fight, when should the police be called?**
   A. Whenever a situation has become potentially violent
   B. After separating the guests who are fighting
   C. After calming down the guests who are fighting
   D. After physically restraining the guests who are fighting

10. **You witness a drug transaction on the premises. You should**
    A. call the police.
    B. ignore the situation to prevent a possible confrontation.
    C. do nothing if the transaction occurred outside the building.
    D. warn the offenders that you are going to inform your manager.

For answers, please turn to page 4-22.

ANSWERS

Page	Activity

4-2 Test Your Knowledge

1. False 2. False 3. True 4. False 5. False

4-6 Am I Saying That Right?

1. Yes. The statement is phrased as an "I" statement and is not judgmental, which helps deflect blame from the guest. It also offers the guest a nonalcoholic alternative.
2. No. Service is being stopped to the guest as the last drink is being served. It's best to wait until the guest orders the next round before telling him or her that you are stopping service.
3. No. This statement is judgmental. It would be better to leave it at, *"It's against our policy to serve you any more alcohol."*
4. Yes. The statement is phrased as an "I" statement and is not judgmental.
5. No. This statement is judgmental and is likely to provoke a confrontation.
6. No. While this statement sounds as though the person is expressing concern, it is actually judgmental. It would be better to say something like, *"I want to make sure you get home safely, so I am not able to serve you."*
7. No. This statement is definitely judgmental and could provoke an incident.
8. No. It sounds as though the guest has convinced the bartender or server to serve another drink after the decision was made to stop service. You must be firm and not change your mind once the decision has been made to stop service.
9. Yes. You should always try to enlist the help of an accompanying guest when stopping service.
10. Yes. The statement is phrased as an "I" statement and is not judgmental. It is appropriate to quote the law when stopping service.

4-15 Rate the Response

1. Rating: 1—Effective

   Here is how the hostess, the server, and the manager handled the situation effectively:
   - The hostess correctly informed the server about the signs of intoxication exhibited by the guest.
   - The server asked the hostess to alert the manager about the situation.
   - The server's statements were not judgmental when refusing alcohol service to the guest. He was also empathetic.
   - The server quoted the law when denying service.
   - The hostess called the police.
   - The hostess and server moved other guests away from the situation when the guest became violent.
   - The manager intervened when the guest became violent.
2. Rating: 1—Effective

   Here is how the server, the bus person, and the maitre d' handled the situation effectively:
   - The bus person alerted the server that her guests were exhibiting signs of intoxication.
   - The server alerted the maitre d' as a backup.
   - The server was not judgmental when informing the guest of her decision to stop service.
   - The server deflected blame from the guest to company policy.
   - The server expressed concern when stopping service.
   - The server was firm in her decision about stopping service.
   - The maitre d' was close enough to observe, but did not appear threatening to the guests.

Continued on next page...

ANSWERS continued

Page Activity

3. Rating: 1—Effective

   Here is how the valet handled the situation effectively:

   - The valet was firm but not judgmental.
   - The valet was empathetic and expressed concern for the guest's safety.
   - The valet threatened to call the police when the guest insisted on driving.
   - The valet arranged for alternate transportation.

4. Rating: 3—Ineffective

   The bartender made the following mistakes:

   - The bartender failed to inform the manager about the potential of a fight before it occurred, even though there were definite signs that the situation was escalating.
   - The bartender failed to call the police when the guests began fighting.
   - The bartender separated the two fighting guests and physically restrained one of them. The bartender also restrained a guest from leaving the establishment.
   - The bartender failed to separate other guests from the situation.

5. Rating: 3—Ineffective

   The bartender made the following mistakes:

   - The bartender used judgmental, disrespectful statements when stopping service.
   - The bartender did not attempt to stop the intoxicated woman from leaving the establishment.

6. Rating: 2—Somewhat effective

   Here is why the bartender was only somewhat effective:

   - The bartender's statements when attempting to stop service were not judgmental.
   - The bartender was empathetic and expressed concern.
   - The bartender offered the guest nonalcoholic alternatives.
   - The bartender did not, however, stick with the decision to stop service. Serving alcohol to an intoxicated guest is illegal.

7. Rating: 2—Somewhat effective

   Here is why the server and the bartender were only somewhat effective:

   - Their initial statements when stopping service were judgmental.
   - The bartender tried to recover by deflecting blame for stopping service to the potential loss of the establishment's liquor license and being fired.
   - The bartender asked how the intoxicated guest was getting home. It is unclear whether or not his companions were sober.

8. Rating: 2—Somewhat effective

   Here is why the bartender and the manager were only somewhat effective:

   - The bartender was effective because she reported the activity.
   - The manager, however, failed to act on the information and did not call the police.

9. Rating: 3—Ineffective

   The server made the following mistake:

   - The server overserved the guests. Whether or not a designated driver is present, it is illegal to serve an intoxicated guest.

Continued on next page...

ANSWERS continued

Page	Activity

10. Rating: 2—Somewhat effective

    Here is why the server was only somewhat effective:

    - Once the server decided to stop service, the server did not secure a backup.
    - The server initially was not judgmental when stopping service to the guest, and then became judgmental after being insulted.
    - The server expressed concern for the guest's safety.
    - The server was firm in her decision to stop service.
    - Once the server found out the intoxicated guest was receiving drinks from his companions, alcohol service was stopped and all alcohol was removed from the table. She could have put herself in danger since she had no backup.

4-18 Multiple-Choice Study Questions

1. B
2. A
3. B
4. D
5. A
6. C
7. B
8. A
9. A
10. A

NOTES

Index